THE GOD WHO LOVES YOU

PETER KREEFT

THE GOD WHO LOVES YOU

"Love Divine, All Loves Excelling"

IGNATIUS PRESS SAN FRANCISCO

Originally published under the title:
Knowing the Truth of God's Love

Published by Servant Books, Ann Arbor Michigan

Cover art:

Return of the Prodigal Son, 1990
Fouquet (b. 1922)
Private Collection

Design by Roxanne Mei Lum

ISBN 1-58617-017-1
Library of Congress Control Number 2004107664
Printed in the United States of America ♾

In memory of
Sheldon Vanauken

"In the twilight of our lives,
we will be judged on how we have loved."
— St. John of the Cross

CONTENTS

INTRODUCTION

Why write a book about God's love? Why read it?

"God loves you"—isn't that the most well-worn of clichés? It's just standard filler for the laziest, most obvious and repetitive homilies. Smile. Yawn. Everybody knows that by now, at least everybody who has ever been in a church or read a Bible.

No. Exactly the opposite. It is *not* familiar. It is shattering. It changes everything. And most Christians do not realize it.

The Bible does not tell us what we already know. For instance, not once does it argue for God's existence. We already know that by reason or experience or history or science or logic or common sense. Only "the fool has said in his heart, 'There is no God.'" (Ps 14:1). But it does tell us what we do not already know: the *nature* of God. We do not know that "God is love" by reason or experience or history or science or logic or common sense. That is a shock.

We think we have absorbed that shock, since it hit the earth 2,000 years ago. But we have not. The shock waves have not diminished. They are still hitting us, but we are not feeling them.

Not only do we not know what God is until God shocks us, we also do not know what "love" really means until God's love shocks us. If the original shock has worn off, see Mel Gibson's movie *The Passion of the Christ*. That will show you what love really means.

This book is an attempt to listen to those shock waves.

But *how* could such a book be written?

There is only one valid way to write a book about love: out of love. And there is only one valid way to write a book about the love of God: out of the love of God.

So the reason for the existence of this book is the same as the reason for the existence of the universe. God loved the universe into existence. And I loved this book into existence.

But I am not a great lover of God, but a mediocre one. So why should you read my book? Why learn love from a mediocre lover?

The primary book about God's love is the Bible, of course, and no book can replace that, just as no building can replace the earth that all buildings stand on. But there are also hundreds of other books about God's love written by great lovers of God: the saints. Read them, of course. But why read mine too? Why listen to a plodder in the valley when there are saints on the mountaintops?

First reason: Because the plodding pilgrim in the valley can at least see the mountain and appreciate its grandeur from a distance and call out to other pilgrims to tell them of the heights. Beginners appreciate books by other beginners.

Second reason: The Bible is like the ocean, the saints' books are like rivers, and mine is like a tiny, babbling brook, but all are made of the same water.

Third reason: because even a tiny bit of new insight into the greatest thing is more valuable than enormous new knowledge of tiny things. And next to God's love, everything is tiny.

Fourth reason: I have written almost fifty books, and everything in every one of them might be mistaken, but this one thing has to be true: that God is love.

Fifth reason: Because nothing is more joyful, more liberating, than that. If you could keep only one piece of divine revelation, and had to lose all the others, this would be the one to keep.

Sixth reason: because nothing more powerfully hastens you on your journey toward your appointed end, the end for which you were created, namely to become a saint. For a saint is simply a great lover of God, and nothing elicits love more than love. "Everybody loves a lover." Nothing makes us saints faster than being hit over the head with God's love.

That's why I wrote this book.

But how can anyone write a book about God's love? Isn't that like trying to put the sun in a suitcase?

> If all the seas with ink would fill
> And were the skies of parchment made,
> Were every pen on earth a quill
> And every man a scribe by trade,
> To write the love of God above
> Would drain the oceans dry,
> Nor could the whole contain the scroll
> Though stretched from sky to sky.

This is true. There is no answer to this last objection. Except that if I kept silence, the very stones would cry out.

I

The Twelve Most Profound Ideas I Have Ever Had

The twelve most profound ideas I have ever discovered all concern the love of God.

None of them is original. But every one is revolutionary. None of them came *from* me. But all of them came *to* me with sudden force and fire: the "aha!" experience, the "eureka!" experience. They were all *realizations*, not just beliefs.

1. **There is only "one thing necessary".** The first happened when I was about six or seven, I think. It was the first important conscious religious discovery I ever made, and I do not think I have ever had a maturer or wiser thought than that one. I remember to this day exactly where I was when it hit me: riding north on Haledon Avenue between Sixth and Seventh Streets in Paterson, New Jersey, after Sunday morning church with my parents. Isn't it remarkable how we remember exactly where we were when great events happen that change our lives?

I had learned some things about God and Jesus, about Heaven, and about good and evil in church and Sunday school. Like most children at that age, I was a bit confused and overwhelmed by it all, especially by what this great Being called God expected of me. I felt a little insecure,

I guess, about not knowing and a little guilty about not doing everything that I was supposed to be doing. Then all of a sudden the sun shone through the fog. I saw the one thing necessary that made sense and order out of everything else.

I checked out my insight with my father, my most reliable authority. He was an elder in the church and (much more important) a good and wise man. "Dad, everything they teach us in church and Sunday school, all the stuff we're supposed to learn from the Bible—it all comes down to only one thing, doesn't it? I mean, if we only remember the one most important thing all the time, then all the other things will be okay, right?"

He was rightly skeptical. "What one thing? There are a lot of things that are important."

"I mean, I should just always ask what God wants me to do and then do it. That's all, isn't it?"

Wise men know when they've lost an argument. "You know, I think you're right, Son. That's it."

I had perceived—via God's grace, not my own wit, surely—that since God *is* love, we must therefore love God and love whatever God loves; that if we turn to the divine Conductor and follow the wise and loving baton that is His will, His Word, then the music of our life will be a symphony.

2. The way to happiness is self-forgetful love. A second realization follows closely upon this one. That is, it follows logically. But it did not follow closely in time for me. Instead, it took half a lifetime to appreciate, through a million experiments, every one of which proved the same result: that the way to happiness is self-forgetful love and the way to unhappiness is self-regard, self-worry, and the search for personal happiness. Our happiness comes to us only when we do not seek for it. It comes to us when we seek others' happiness instead.

It is an embarrassingly common lesson to take so long to learn, but most of us are incredibly slow learners. We constantly try other ways, thinking that perhaps the happiness that did not come to us the last time through selfishness will do so next time. It never does. The truth is blindingly clear, but we are clearly blind.

The secret of love is not hidden, for "God is love", and God is not hidden. God said through His prophet Isaiah: "I did not speak in secret, / in a land of darkness; / I did not say to the offspring of Jacob, / 'Seek me in chaos.' / I the LORD speak the truth, / I declare what is right" (Is 45:19).

Of course God's secret plans, which we do not need to know, are hidden. And God's infinite nature, which finite minds cannot know, is hidden. But the thing that we need to know, God does not hide from us. He offers it to us publicly and freely. Jesus invited prospective disciples to "come and see" (Jn 1:39). We are told by the Apostle Paul to "test everything; hold fast what is good" (1 Thess 5:21).

This lesson is so well known that even a pagan like Buddha at least knew its negative half. His "second noble truth" is that the source of all unhappiness and suffering (*dukkha*) is selfishness (*tanha*). All who teach the opposite—that selfishness is the way to happiness—are unhappy souls. "By their fruits you shall know them", as Jesus tells us. Who are the happiest people on earth? People like Mother Teresa's sisters who have nothing, give everything and "rejoice in the Lord always" (Phil 4:4).

3. "In everything God works for good with those who love him." A third shattering realization was that Romans 8:28 was literally true: "In everything God works for good with those who love him." This is surely the most astonishing verse in the Bible, for it certainly does not *look* as if all things work for good. What awful things our lives contain! But if God, the all-powerful Creator and Designer and Provider of our lives, is 100 percent love, then it necessarily follows, as the night the day, that everything in His world, from birth to death, from kisses to slaps, from candy to cancer, comes to us out of God's active or permissive love.

It is incredibly simple and perfectly reasonable. It is only our complexity that makes it look murky. As G.K. Chesterton says, life is always complicated for someone without principles. Here is the shining simplicity: *if God is total love, then everything He wills for me must come from his love and be for my good.* For that is what love is, the willing of the beloved's good. And if this God of sheer love is also omnipotent and can do anything He wills, then it follows that all things must work together for my ultimate good.

Not necessarily for my *immediate* good, for short-range harm may be the necessary road to long-range good. And not necessarily for my *apparent* good, for appearances may be deceiving. Thus suffering does not *seem* good. But it can always work for my real and ultimate good. Even the bad things I and others do, though they do not come from God, are allowed by God because they are included in His plan. You cannot checkmate, corner, surprise, or beat Him. "He's got the whole world in His hands." And He's got my whole life in His hands, too. He could take away any evil—natural, human, or demonic—like swatting a fly. He allows it only because it works out for our greater good in the end, just as it did with Job.

In fact, every atom in the universe moves exactly as it does only because omnipotent Love designed it so. Dante was right: it is "the love that moves the sun and all the stars".

This is not poetic fancy but sober, logical fact. Therefore, the most profound thing you can say really is this simple children's grace for meals: "God is great and God is good; let us thank Him for our food. Amen!"

I had always believed in God's love and God's omnipotence. But once I put the two ideas together, saw the unavoidable logical conclusion (Rom 8:28), and applied this truth to my life, I could never again see the world the same way. If God is great (omnipotent) and God is good (loving), then everything that happens is our spiritual food; and we should thank Him for it.

4. Everything is a gift from God. A fourth revolutionary insight follows closely upon the third: everything is a gift. Nature, people, things, events—all the things in our lives that we take for granted—are granted to us and given to us actively and deliberately by God the giver.

This gives us a whole new way of looking at things. We usually see them as only *things*. But they are *signs*. A sign is not only a thing, but it also has another level of meaning. For instance, a road sign on a metal post along the roadway is first of all a thing, but it is also a sign. As a thing, it *is* simply a flat metal surface with a painted design of some sort placed along the roadway. But as a sign, it *means* something else. It means what it points to. For instance, it might tell us New York City is forty miles away in a certain direction.

When we give a gift, it is not only a thing but also a sign of something: a sign of our love perhaps. We want the recipients of our gifts not only to get things—like candy or flowers—but also "to get the message". We communicate that we care about them enough to give them a gift.

All the things in this world are gifts and signs. As gifts, they point beyond themselves to the divine Giver. As signs, they point beyond themselves to the God they signify and reveal, as a letter reveals the writer. And since God is love, the one thing everything signifies is God's love to us. The whole world is a love letter from God.

Bernard of Clairvaux, a Doctor of the Church and a great lover of God, said that when he looked at a crucifix, the wounds of Christ seemed like lips speaking to him and saying, "I love you." Everything is like that. Everything is God's lips speaking love. That is God's message to us in every thing. Everything has its meaning *between* God and us, not in itself. Everything is relative to this absolute.

This way of looking at things, as gifts and signs rather than simply as things in themselves, is not our usual way of seeing. Try this new way for just one hour and see the difference it makes. See the sunrise not as a mindless, mechanical necessity but as God's smile. See a wave not just as tons of cold salt water crashing down on the shore but as God's playful action. See even death as not just a biological necessity but as God tucking us in at bedtime so that we can rise to new life in the morning.

This is not a trick we play on ourselves or a fantasy. This is what the world really is. It is just as true to say that every snowflake is a gift of God as it is true to say that every cent in a father's inheritance is a gift to his children. It is just as true to say that every leaf on every tree is a work of art made by the divine Artist with the intention that we see it, know it, love it, and rejoice in it, as it is true to say that every word in a lover's letter to his beloved is meant to be seen, known, loved, and enjoyed. This is not fantasy. What is fantasy is the horrible habit the modern world has gotten itself into, the habit of thinking that what the world really is is only atoms and chance, only what the senses and science reveal and everything else is mere subjective fancy.

5. God did it all for me alone. The realization that God's love for me is bigger and more cosmic than we can ever imagine was complemented by the realization that it is also more intimate and personal than we can ever imagine. This entire cosmic drama was, in God's plan, there *for me*. And for every other member of His body, His family. Everything God ever did—the creation of the universe, amazing miracles, and the universal laws by which He moves history forward—the Big Bang, the Incarnation, and the law of gravity—are there not for the universe or even for "humanity". No, they are there for you and me.

If I had been the only one created, as one of the saints says, God would have done no less. He would have gone to all this trouble, even death on the Cross, for me alone. In fact, it is not just that He *would* have done it all for me alone, but that He *did* do it all for me alone. The Cross has my name on it. His intention did not go out to an anonymous mass of humanity with me simply included as a member of the species. His love letter to me does not come addressed: "Dear Occupant". He gathers his sheep one by one, calling each *by name* (Jn 10:1–3). A name is a "proper noun", not a "common noun". Your name is uniquely yours. He knows you by name because that is what love is: intimate, personal knowledge of the beloved. That is why Scripture has used the word *know* for the monogamous marriage relationship. That is why marriage is used to symbolize our relationship to God.

Jesus never loved the conceptual abstraction called humanity, nor did He ever tell us to. He told us to love our real neighbor, the person who is there and who by being there makes real and inconvenient demands on us. Loving our neighbor means laying down our will for him, as God laid down His will for us.

6. We will be perfectly and uniquely fulfilled by God's love in Heaven. Since love is always directed toward the individual person and since God's love for me is unique, Heaven—the perfection and consummation of this special love relationship—must be altogether unique for each person. Each of us in Heaven will have our own "mansion" or suite of rooms into which God will enter in an absolutely unique way.

I am deeply moved by C. S. Lewis' chapter on Heaven in *The Problem of Pain*, especially by what he says about the scriptural symbol of the "white stone":

> "To him that overcometh I will give a white stone, and in the stone a new name written, which no man knoweth saving he that receiveth it." What can be more a man's own than this new name which even in eternity remains a secret between God and him? And what shall we take this secrecy to mean? Surely, that each of the redeemed shall forever know and praise some one aspect of the divine beauty better than any other creature can. Why else were individuals created, but that God, loving all infinitely, should love each differently? And this difference, so far from impairing, floods with meaning the love of all blessed creatures for one another, the communion of saints.... For doubtless the continually successful, yet never completed, attempt by each soul to communicate its unique vision to all others (and that by means whereof earthly art and philosophy are but clumsy imitations) is also among the ends for which the individual was created.[1]

All my life I search for this unique, individual self—my true self—and yet I never fully find it. Only God knows it fully,

[1] C. S. Lewis, *The Problem of Pain* (New York: Macmillan Publishing, 1962), pp. 149–50.

for He designed it. And only God can give it to me because He created it and is creating it right now, sculpting it with all the tools of heredity and environment that make up my life. None of us knows who we really are once we stop fooling ourselves. That knowledge and that destiny await us in our home. Our home is in Heaven because our true identity as individuals is waiting for us there. The character's identity is found in the author's mind and nowhere else.

7. The gift of God's love is ours for the taking. I am a Roman Catholic. But the most liberating idea I have ever heard I first learned from Martin Luther. Pope John Paul II told the German Lutheran bishops that Luther was profoundly right about this idea. He said that Catholic teaching affirms it just as strongly and that there was no contradiction between Protestant and Catholic theology on this terribly important point, which was the central issue of the Protestant Reformation. I speak, of course, about "justification by faith" and its consequence, which Luther called "Christian liberty" or "the liberty of a Christian" in his little gem of an essay by that name.

Let us be careful to approach the point in the right way. I think most misunderstandings begin at this very first step. Let's begin with a solid certainty: God is love. God is a lover, not a manager, businessman, accountant, owner, or puppet-master. What He wants from us first of all is not a technically correct performance but our heart. Protestants and Catholics alike need to relearn or reemphasize that simple, liberating truth. When I first read C. S. Lewis' statement of it in *Mere Christianity*, I was a Protestant. But it liberated me just as it had the Catholic Augustinian monk Luther 450 years earlier. The crucial sentence for me was: "We may think God wants actions of a certain kind, but God wants people of a certain sort."

The point is amazingly simple, which is why so many of us just don't get it. Heaven is free because love is free. It is ours for the taking. The taking is faith. "If you believe, you will be saved." It is really that simple. If I offer you a gift, you have it if and only if you have the faith to take it.

The primacy of faith does not discount or denigrate works but liberates them. Our good works can now also be free—free from the worry and slavery and performance anxiety of having to buy Heaven with them. Our good works can now flow from genuine love of neighbor, not fear of Hell. Nobody wants to be loved merely as a means to build up the lover's merit pile. That attempt is ridiculous logically as well as psychologically. How much does Heaven cost? A thousand good works? Would 999 not do, then? The very question shows its own absurdity. That absurdity comes from forgetting that God is love.

God practices what He preaches. He loves the sinner and hates only the sin. The father of the prodigal son did not say to his repentant son: "You are welcome home, Son, but of course you must now pay me back for all the harm you've done and all the money you've wasted." He didn't even say, "I hope you've learned your lesson." He simply fell on his neck, kissed him, and wept.

The righteous older brother was scandalized by this apparently unjust justification of the sinner—just as the day-long laborers in another of Christ's strange and wonderful parables were scandalized when the master of the vineyard gave the same wage he had given them to the late arrivals. So too the people who heard Jesus forgive the repentant thief on the cross were probably scandalized by the words: "Today you will be with me in Paradise." They probably thought, "But what about all his past sins? What about justice? What about punishment?" The answer is found in 1 John 4:18:

"There is no fear in love, but perfect love casts out fear. For fear has to do with punishment."

God cannot be outdone in loving us lavishly. No one can even imagine how loving God is: "Eye hath not seen, nor ear heard, neither have entered into the heart of man, the things which God hath prepared for them that love him" (1 Cor 2:9 KJV). The prodigal son did not find himself in the servants' quarters but in the banquet hall. He had hoped his father might consent to take him back as one of his hired servants, but he was dressed in festal robes and fed the fatted calf.

The whole point of justification by faith is God's scandalous, crazy, and wonderful gift of love.

8. Because of the love of God, we can love our neighbor freely. Another infinitely precious discovery came in the same package as the previous one. Flowing from the insight of justification by faith, which is about our vertical relationship with God, came this associated insight about our horizontal relationship with our neighbor: because we have received a new kind of love from God (*agape*), we can love our neighbor in a new way. We can love our neighbor freely without "performance anxiety", without worrying about results. We can now love, not *for* success or gratification or happiness or fulfillment, but *from* God's love. We can love others not from need but from sheer bounty, just as we have been loved. We become channels of this new living water. We freely pass on this tremendous gift we have received.

When we love for some desired end, we are slaves to anxiety and worry about attainment. We "hanker after the fruits", to quote Gandhi, and this hankering is necessarily fearful and anxious. Jesus offers a radically different way, as Gandhi found in the Gospels: "Be anxious for nothing" (Mt 6:25–34).

Not even for whether our love works or not. As Mother Teresa of Calcutta often said, "God does not call us to be successful, but to be faithful." We are to love *out of* God and therefore out of success, rather than *for* success. We must live from our end and not just for it. For "it is finished." The battle has already been won by God's love. Our love is only the mop-up operation.

We need not worry about success because our love is guaranteed success, even if it does not move our neighbor to respond. For if we are one with Christ as members of His body, then our love is part of Christ's love. It is not just an imitation from afar but a participation from within. And Christ's love is guaranteed success, even though it was crucified in us and often continues to be crucified by the world. It is guaranteed success not because of its intentions or goals, but because of where it comes from: the Son's perfect obedience to the Father.

The question keeps coming up in John's Gospel: Where does this man Jesus come from? Does He come from God or only from man? The question is the most basic one that can be asked about us and our love. Are we and our love born again from above, from God? Or are we and it only the product of human nature? The answer to this question makes an infinite difference, the difference between Heaven and Hell in the next life. It also makes the difference in this life between the holy happiness of living and loving *from* God's fullness versus the agonizing anxiety of living and loving *for* fullness only as an ideal but out of a deep emptiness and need, for that is what we find in the fallen human heart.

The most liberating discovery is that since God has filled us with His own life, our loving can be like a tube open at both ends, with God's love coming in one end and out the other, in by faith and out by works. The alternative is to be a tube open at only one end, the neighbor's end. Then we try to squeeze our own toothpaste out of the tube. But we have only a finite amount of spiritual toothpaste to give. So we worry about squandering it, just as the older brother in the parable of the prodigal son did. But God's supply is infinite. That's why the saints love so recklessly. It is not their love they love with, but God's.

9. God's love is an objective reality that makes a real difference. The foundation for understanding this infinite love of God, in turn, is another closely related big idea. It is an idea that I was amazed to discover most Christians today do not understand, though in previous centuries it was always viewed as central to the Christian life. The truth put simply is that God's love is not a mere feeling or attitude inside Him. No, it is an objective reality that causes a real effect outside God and in us. Just as God's Word (His *Logos* or mind) is not merely subjective in the Father but is eternally begotten as another divine person, the Son, so the love of the Father and the Son is not just a subjective reality in Them but eternally proceeds as another divine person, the Holy Spirit.

God's love is as objective as light. Because the sun in a sense *is* light, or the source of light rather than being lit, it really gives its light to the earth. And because the earth really receives light from the sun, it is really transformed every morning from darkness to light. Just as objectively, because God *is* love, God really gives love to us. And because we receive real life-changing love from God, we are really transformed from darkness to light. It is not a mere change in subjective attitude but in our objective being. We are "born again". We receive a new life, a kind of spiritual blood transfusion from God. It is not physical blood, but it is just as real. We receive *life* from God's love, not just a lifestyle. "If any one is in Christ, he is a new creation" (2 Cor 5:17).

Once again it was C. S. Lewis who taught me this. Outside the New Testament, I have never read any better summary of what it means to be a Christian than Lewis' *Mere Christianity*, especially Part IV, in which he talks about this objective reality of the new birth.

Repeatedly, I ask my students: "What is a Christian?" And repeatedly they answer only in terms of beliefs, feelings, or deeds. "A Christian is one who believes the teachings of Christ." Ah, but "even the demons believe—and shudder" (Jas 2:19). "A Christian is someone who trusts Christ." Then being a Christian depends on how trusting I feel toward God? "A Christian is someone who follows Christ's way of life or tries to." How many good deeds make you a Christian, then?

The answer is not only what a Christian believes or feels or does. A Christian is a different being, a new creature with a whole new nature. A Christian has been *born again*. Unfortunately, even this incomparably profound metaphor from the lips of Christ Himself is often trivialized and subjectivized. It is reduced to mean a mere experience or feeling. But it is not first of all a feeling, but a fact. When a baby is born, the birth occurs whether the baby feels it or not.

It is God's love that gives us our new birth. God's love is the cause. It is also the effect in us. For the effect of the new birth is that we now have a share in our Father's nature, which *is* love.

Letting God into my soul by faith changes not just my attitudes but also my being, as a wife's acceptance of her husband's sexual advances can change not just her attitude but her being: it can make her pregnant. Faith means choosing to say "yes" to God's desire to impregnate our souls. Faith means being pregnant with God's life, which is divine overflowing love. Thus God's love is both the origin and the end, the cause and the effect, the Alpha and the Omega of our Christian life. That's why that life in Scripture is repeatedly referred to as a spiritual marriage relationship with God.

10. We were made to be united to God forever. The next link in the chain of big ideas follows as closely as the previous ones. If faith is being pregnant with God's love in this life, then Heaven is like our spiritual birthday. As a man plants his seed in a woman, the new life is planted in our souls by grace. As the seed grows and takes shape in the womb as a baby, our Christian life on earth grows and takes shape through God's grace in the womb of our souls. We are being prepared for glory. And as physical birth is the full flowering of the "planted" baby, our heavenly life is the blossoming of this divine seed planted in our souls.

Or to use another metaphor, our faith on earth is a solemn engagement and Heaven is the marriage. Our destiny is to be so intimately united with God that, as the mystics say, we not only see God's face but also see *with* God's face. We share in His own consciousness and love. Here on earth, too, personal intimacy, whether in marriage or in a lasting friendship, means not just being close to the other person as an object, but sharing his or her own thoughts and feelings, having a common outlook on life, a common face.

For this union the very stars were made. For this union God came an infinite distance from Heaven to earth, from divine glory to humiliation, from holy purity and innocence to a criminal's death on a cross, from perfect oneness with the Father to the Hell of being forsaken by the Father—all this just to marry us. And for this marriage God brought us an infinite distance, too. First He brought us from nothing into being by creation and by providentially guiding every atom in the universe in a cosmic dance to bring us to birth. (For the universe is like a great mother.) Then He brought us another infinite distance, from flesh to spirit, from Adam to New Adam, from damnation to salvation, by the new birth. God took all this double trouble, this infinite trouble—for what? For the consummation of His marriage with us. And why? Because God is love, and perfect union is the goal of love.

This is the ultimate reason for the creation of the universe. Whenever we love God, whenever we turn from self-will to God's will, whenever we say "yes" to God's love, the whole universe rejoices and is consummated. *That* is what "the whole creation has been groaning in travail together" about (Rom 8:22). We can fulfill or frustrate the deepest longing of the stars. We are the priests of the universe.

11. The desire for joy points us to the love of God. This destiny explains another "big idea": the mysterious longing that C. S. Lewis writes about so movingly and calls "Joy". It is the most memorable and arresting theme in all his writing. Nothing ever moved him more. Any reader who has ever experienced it feels the same way: "No one who has ever experienced it would ever exchange it for all the happiness in the world" (*Surprised by Joy*).

"Joy", says Lewis, "is a technical term" (thus he capitalizes it) "and must be distinguished from both pleasure and happiness." "Joy" in Lewis' sense is not a satisfaction, but a desire. But he calls it "Joy" because though it is a dissatisfaction, it is more satisfying, more joyful, than any other satisfaction. This is one of its two distinctive qualities. The other is its mystery. Its object—the thing desired—is indefinable and unattainable, at least in this life.

Nevertheless that object must be real, Lewis argues, for the desire is innate and every innate desire corresponds to some reality. Where there is hunger, there is somewhere real food that can satisfy it. If there is thirst, there must be water. And if there is divine discontent with earth even at its best, there must be a Heaven.

The explanation for this mysterious desire is Augustine's great sentence: "Thou hast made us for Thyself, and [therefore] our hearts are restless until they rest in Thee" (*Confessions* I,1). The reason for our restless lover's quarrel with the world is that we are engaged to God, not to the world. "He has made everything beautiful in its time; also he has put eternity into man's mind", says Ecclesiastes (3:11). Our souls are God-shaped vacuums, and "this infinite abyss can only be filled with an infinite and eternal object, i.e., by God", explains the French philosopher and scientist Blaise Pascal in the *Pensées*. This desire is God's footprint in the sands of the soul. This discontent with known earthly joy, this longing for an unknown joy more than earth can ever offer, is the most moving thing in our lives because it is really our longing and love for God, whether we know it or not.

12. Romantic love reveals the beloved and is meant to point us toward union with God. The only possible rival to joy for the title of the most moving and precious experience in our lives is romantic love. Indeed, to many people who have repressed or misunderstood their innate longing for God, romantic love is the only momentous and moving mystery they know. How else could a face ever launch a thousand ships?

Those who understand joy know why romantic love moves us: because it is an image of joy. It is joy horizontalized, with the earthly beloved standing for God in either of two very different ways: either it is substituted for God as an idol, or else it reflects and mediates the love of God, as in the Dante-Beatrice relationship in *La Vita Nuova*.

In the first case, love is not only blind but also blinding, like all idolatries and all addictions. It is mistaking a creature for God, treating it as an absolute, as absolutely necessary to my happiness. But in the second case, love is not blind but perfectly accurate. In fact, the highest and most precise accuracy is found here. Love is our most perfect knowledge.

We see this principle reflected in Scripture. The bridegroom in Solomon's Song of Songs is traditionally interpreted as God the lover of our souls. We are His bride. But this divine Bridegroom says to the human bride: "You are all fair, my love" (4:7). God says this to us!

But how can it be true that we are "all fair" when we still struggle with sin? Is God blind? If not, then what He says must be true. It is true as prophecy, a prophecy of our eternal identity and destiny. Christ refers to this when He says, "You, therefore, must be perfect, as your heavenly Father is perfect" (Mt 5:48). God speaks from eternity and sees us as we are eternally before Him. To us, this "all fair" perfection is only in the future. But to God everything is present. For that is what eternity is: not endless futures but all times actually present with no dead past or unborn future, no "no longer" or "not yet".

Whether we understand this or not, whether we can conceive eternity or not, one thing is clear: God is love and God is not blind, which means that love is not blind. Not this kind of love, not *agape*. (See Chapter Three for a definition of *agape*.)

Romantic love can be blind. It can be only *eros*. Or it can be a sharing in this *agape* kind of love. When it is the latter, it penetrates to the mysterious center of the beloved's being and perceives—at least unconsciously—her incalculable worth, because it sees her not as an object, but as a subject, as an *I*. Every object, every *thing*, has a finite value that can be calculated quantitatively or qualitatively. But the *I* is not an object. The value of the *I* not calculable. That is because the human *I* is made in the image of God whose essential name is "I AM".

Love sees this implicitly. Because love does not look from without but from within, it sees really and clearly. Love sees eye to eye because it sees I to I. "The heart has its reasons which the reason does not know", says Pascal in the *Pensées*. This is not sentimentality: the heart has its *reasons*. The heart *sees*. Love sees. It is this new vision that excites and moves us so mysteriously in romantic love, not just blind animal desire. Love glimpses a new world.

Jesus knows this. That is why He says, "Blessed are the pure in heart, for they shall see God" (Mt 5:8). As the nineteenth-century Danish religious philosopher Søren Kierkegaard tells us in the title of one of his books: *Purity of Heart Is to Will One Thing*. It is to obey "the great and first commandment": "You shall love the Lord your God with all your heart, and with all your soul, and with all your mind" (Mt 22:37–38). Only when we have this purity of heart and love can we understand God. God is a person, and the only way to understand a person is by love, and the only way to perfect understanding is by perfect love.

We all know this principle innately. Whom do you trust to understand you best: one who loves you or one who does not? Who understands you best: someone with a large heart or someone with a large head? Is it the one who loves you deeply but is not terribly bright? Or is it the one who is terribly bright but does not love you? The genius may know more things about you, but only the lover knows you, for genius knows things, but love knows persons.

Romantic love is love of one special, unique individual. This love is not a command or a duty like love of neighbor. It has no moral merit. We fall into it as into a hole. It is a gift and a glory. It is like Heaven that way: Heaven too is a gift and a glory, not a payment. All talk of merit and law and obedience—necessary as it is on earth—will disappear in Heaven, except perhaps as a joke. Romantic love is God's sample of Heaven strewn along our earthly pilgrimage. *Eros* is the appetizer for *agape*.

These are, I think, the twelve most profound ideas I have ever had. However, there is one idea that I have heard that I think is even more profound. It is Karl Barth's answer to the questioner who asked him, "Professor Barth, you have written dozens of great books, and many of us think you are the greatest theologian in the world. Of all your many ideas, what is the most profound thought you have ever had?" Without a second's hesitation, the great theologian replied, "Jesus loves me."

2

The Point of It All

John, the youngest of Jesus' disciples, was the last to die. As he grew older his teaching grew simpler, as you can see by reading his first Epistle. He spoke always and only of one thing: the love of God. According to an old tradition, one of his disciples complained to him about this: "Why don't you talk about anything else?" He answered, "Because there isn't anything else."

Christianity is both complex and simple. Some religions are simple like Buddhism, which according to Buddha himself is nothing but the Four Noble Truths. Or take Islam, which is clear-cut and simple as the desert sun. On the other hand, some religions are complex like Hinduism with its many different deities and yogas. C. S. Lewis makes a distinction between "thin" (simple, rational) religions and "thick" (complex, mysterious) religions. He compares religions to soups. Some are like consommé: clear and clean and thin like water. Others are like lentil soup or minestrone: thick and dark like blood. Christianity is both. It is full of mysteries like the Trinity, creation, the Incarnation, atonement, providence, and eschatology. In fact, it is the most mysterious religion in the world. It is not at all obvious, not what we would expect. That is what all the heresies have been: what the human mind naturally expected. Yet Christianity is also supremely simple. John was right. There is, in the last analysis, only one thing: the love of God.

Christianity is like a wheel as big and as complex as the cosmos. And the love of God is its hub. Everything else is a spoke. The love of God is the point, the final explanation, of everything else in Christianity and in fact of everything else in the cosmos. The love of God is not just one point among many. It is the ultimate cause and reason, the meaning and explanation for everything else. For everything that exists, exists only because of God's will to create, preserve, provide for, guide, and complete it. And God's will is absolutely simple and single in motive: "God *is* love" (1 Jn 4:8).

Love Has Infinite Value

That is why love has infinite value. The entire finite universe disappears like a speck when placed on the scales of value next to the love of God. That is what the Apostle Paul says in a passage that contains a shocking word. Very few Christians know this word is in the Bible because the newer translations cover it up with euphemisms. It is a disgusting word. But in the context in which Paul uses it, it is a wonderful and even a liberatingly hilarious word. The word is *skubala*.

Here is the context. Paul is comparing values, playing the game they teach you in modern ethical discussions. He is prioritizing his values, arranging them in a hierarchical order. He is comparing his life before Christ came into it with his life afterward. His life in Christ was full of persecutions, beatings, shipwrecks, whippings, stonings, and eventually martyrdom. His life before Christ had been full of privileges and worldly success. He was a Roman citizen, educated under Israel's greatest teacher, Gamaliel, "the light of Israel". Paul was "a Hebrew born of Hebrews; as to the law a Pharisee, as to zeal a persecutor of the church, as to righteousness under the law blameless" (Phil 3:5–6). But all these things he calls *skubala* "in order that I may gain Christ" (3:8). "Indeed I count everything as loss because of the surpassing worth of knowing Christ" (3:8).

Do you know what *skubala* means? The old King James Bible had the guts to translate it literally: "dung". You know what that is!

Only a lover of the greater *can* despise the lesser, but only a lover of the lesser has a *right* to despise the lesser. For you have a right to despise only what you have surpassed. Thus Thomas Aquinas called his great *Summa Theologica* "straw" compared to what God had shown him in a mystical experience. The Apostle Paul was no insensitive, world-weary, short-souled, spiritual dwarf. He prized the things he disdained as *skubala*. Yet compared with the new relationship with God that Christ had given him, they were all *skubala*.

Why? Because the finite cannot compare with the infinite. And what is the infinite? What infinity did Christ give Paul? The answer is simple. He gave Paul the infinite love of God, the love that did not limit itself to law and justice. This is the love that gave up Heaven itself, infinite joy, and willingly embraced even Hell and infinite misery on the Cross. "My God, my God, why hast thou forsaken me?" Jesus cried out, as the full weight of sin and misery bore down upon him (Mt 27:46). All out of love for Paul, for you, and for me.

Bernard of Clairvaux wrote a surpassingly beautiful hymn about the incomparable worth of the love of God in Christ called "Jesus, Thou joy of loving hearts". I think the hymn is one of the most moving in human speech because it came not just from the pen of a great writer but also from the heart of a great lover:

> Jesus, Thou joy of loving hearts,
> Thou Fount of life, Thou Light of men,
> From fullest bliss that earth imparts
> We turn unfilled to Thee again.

Thy truth unchanged hath ever stood;
Thou savest those that on Thee call;
To them that seek Thee thou art good;
To them that find Thee, All in all.

We taste Thee, O Thou living Bread,
And long to feast upon Thee still.
We drink from Thee, the fountainhead,
And thirst our souls from Thee to fill.

Our restless spirits yearn for Thee
Where'er our changeful lot is cast;
Glad when Thy gracious smile we see,
Blest when our faith can hold Thee fast.

O Jesus, ever with us stay;
Make all our moments calm and bright;
Chase the dark night of sin away,
Shed o'er the world Thy holy light.

Another of Bernard's hymns, "Jesus, the very thought of Thee", addresses Christ the Beloved thus:

Jesus, the very thought of Thee
With sweetness fills the breast;
But sweeter far Thy face to see
And in Thy presence rest.

No voice can sing, no heart can frame,
Nor can the memory find,
A sweeter sound than Jesus' Name,
The Savior of mankind.

O hope of every contrite heart;
O joy of all the meek;
To them that fall, how kind Thou art;
How good to those who seek!

But what to those who find? Ah, this—
Nor tongue nor pen can show
The love of Jesus, what it is.
None but His loved ones know.

Jesus, our only joy be Thou,
As Thou our prize wilt be;
In Thee be all our glory now,
And through eternity.

Love Is the Greatest Good

This is the thing the great philosophers all sought after, the *summum bonum*, the greatest good, the "pearl of great value" (Mt 13:46), the "one thing needful" (Lk 10:42), the only thing that quiets our restless heart. No sensitive mind can be ignorant of this quest. No lover of wisdom can claim ignorance of the search for wisdom, only ignorance of the finding, the prize. Christ claims to be, simply and absolutely, *the* answer to the fundamental quest of the human heart. All other candidates for the position of the *summum bonum*—pleasure, power, worldly knowledge, honor, fame, health, wealth, even moral virtue—fail to satisfy the restless heart. Why? Because "Thou hast made us for Thyself". That is why "our hearts are restless until they rest in Thee".

The pagan knew the fact that our hearts are restless, but he did not know the reason. Christianity supplies the reason, the key to the lock, the answer to the puzzle pondered by the great philosophers Socrates, Plato, Aristotle, Cicero, even by Qoheleth in the book of Ecclesiastes. All these thinkers believed in a God, but they were not happy because they did not know God was love. Socrates worshipped the unknown God whom he would not name and knew he did not know. Plato's God was impersonal truth and goodness. Aristotle's God was a cosmic first mover who could be known and loved but who did not know or love us. Cicero's God was only a vague object of "piety". And the God of Ecclesiastes sat unmoving and unknown in Heaven while man's life on earth remained "vanity of vanities, all is vanity".

None of these men could have said what the Apostle Paul said in Philippians 3:6–8. None of them could have been happy to be tortured for their faith and love of God. For none of them knew the God of Jesus Christ. They may have smelled Him from afar, like smelling a delicious meal in a restaurant from the street outside, but they could not find the door to come inside. At least not in this lifetime. We may hope God granted it to them in the next. They sought, but Paul and the other Christians found (or rather were found by) the One who said, "I am the door" (Jn 10:9).

Love Is the Supreme Reality

The love of God is not only the supreme *value*, it is also the supreme *reality*. It is not a mere ideal, a potentiality or a possibility in the future. It is the most real, actual, and present of all realities. God's love is not just the supreme principle of morality but also of metaphysics, of the science of being. It is the answer to the great quest: What most fundamentally *is*?

This makes no sense to the typically modern mind, for that mind is skeptical of all claims to know the true nature of being at all, much less the divine being. The typically modern mind also trivializes love by reducing it to a mere feeling, something that arises in us from our desires, or even our chemistry, rather than an objective reality. To many moderns, it is something that is only a part of us rather than something of which we are a part.

But what else could love be than something that is part of us, you ask?

It could be a god! The ancients suspected this. They didn't know *which* god and mistakenly identified it as Venus or Cupid or Aphrodite rather than Yahweh. But they were far closer to the truth than the modern pagan for whom the only god is the self. Better to think of Love as a false god than as no god at all. At least, then, you know its *size*.

Dante is right: love "moves the sun and all the stars". Gravity is simply love's appearance, or its translation into a material medium. Love is as real, objective, and cosmic as gravity. In fact, love *is* gravity—and plant tropism and animal instinct and human free choice and the very nature of the eternal Trinity. Love is the binding force on every level of existence. It is the One that takes many different forms.

In fact, love is in a sense the very stuff of things and not just the form. Things are made of love, and at the consummation of time only love will remain. Whatever in us is not love will not remain but be burned away by the "consuming fire" of God's love. This is the "kingdom that cannot be shaken" when all that has been made will be shaken and removed "in order that what cannot be shaken may remain" (Heb 12:27–28).

What practical difference does this philosophical point about love's objective reality make?

An infinite difference. For there is an infinite difference between real Christianity and a mere ideology, an abstract ethical code, which turns out to be mostly mush and which is all that many Christian preachers preach, all that many Christian teachers teach, and all that many Christians ever hear and learn today. Real Christianity is the living power of God. Real Christianity is the supernatural fire that burst nonbeing asunder and created the universe, and now it has burst the doors of death asunder and recreated humanity. When God's love is experienced only as an ideal, it is experienced as something abstract. When God's love is experienced as a real force and power, it is experienced as something concrete and real—like a concrete block. It is the difference the Apostle Paul refers to when he says, "Our gospel came to you not only in word, but also in power" (1 Thess 1:5). And again, "The kingdom of God does not consist in talk but in power" (1 Cor 4:20). The word translated "power" here is *dynamis*, from which we get our word "dynamite". How many Christians know that dynamite from experience?

The Living Christ Is the Point of It All

The point of Christianity cannot be contained in words because the point of Christianity is the living Christ. He is not an ancient ideal but a real person here and now, ready to barge in and transform our lives. Being a Christian is more like having your soul possessed by a spirit than having your mind clothed with new beliefs. It is more like being well-possessed than well-dressed. It is like being haunted by the Holy Spirit. We are haunted temples.

The love of God is the answer not only to (1) the quest for the supreme *value*—the *summum bonum*—and to (2) the quest for the supreme *reality*—the fundamental principle of the cosmos—but it is also (3) the answer to a third quest, the quest for life's deepest *meaning* and *purpose*.

Kant said there were ultimately only three important questions:

(1) What can I know?
(2) What should I do?
(3) What may I hope?

What I can know is truth, truth about being. Since the ultimate nature of being is love—either in God or in some creature that reflects God—God's love is the answer to Kant's first question.

Love is also the fundamental value. It is the answer to Kant's second question, "What should I do?" On the two commandments to love God and neighbor "depend all the law and the prophets" (Mt 22:40).

Finally, love also gives my life meaning and purpose. It gives me a goal or a hope to shoot for. Hopelessness means purposelessness. Since the ultimate purpose of my life is to learn to love, love is also my hope.

What to Believe, How to Live, and What to Pray For

Thomas Aquinas said that there are only three things we absolutely need to know, and they correspond nicely with Kant's three questions: what to believe, how to live, and what to pray for. Aquinas then says that the Creed answers the first question, the Commandments answer the second, and the Lord's Prayer answers the third. Therefore if we fully understand just these three things, the Creed, the Commandments, and the Lord's Prayer, we will know everything needful. What do these three things have to do with love?

On close inspection, each article of the Creed, each of the Commandments, and each petition of the Lord's Prayer is a form of love. They can be rightly understood only relative to that center. Let us sample each of them to see how this is so.

"I believe in God the Father almighty, creator of heaven and earth." The point of each word of this first article of the Creed is unlocked by the key of love if we really think about it. "I"—what is the I? What is the center of the self? What most fundamentally determines who I shall be? Answer:

How and what I love. Lovers of God or of self, of good or of evil, of persons or of things—these are different *I's*.

"Believe"—what does it mean to believe? What determines belief? Is it logic and evidence? If so, why don't all believe the same things? The evidence and the logic is public and universally available. No, the key to faith is love. We believe only if we love. Trust is the middle term; only if we love, do we trust; and only if we trust, do we believe.

"In"—what is the difference between just *believing that* and *believing in*? To believe *in* God is to trust Him and to love Him. I believe *that* the sun will appear tomorrow, but I do not believe *in* the sun as I believe in the Son. *Belief that* something is so is just an opinion. I would not die for an opinion. But *belief in* someone is a personal relationship of faith and trust and love. That is worth dying for.

"God"—who is this God we believe in? "God is love."

"The Father"—God is our Father. What does a father do? He loves his children into existence and into maturity.

"Almighty"—why is God almighty? What is the secret of His power? What was the secret of Christ's power? He did not march on Rome with arms. He did not compel anyone's will with miracles. He did not even save Himself from death on a cross. Yet no man ever had more power over the human race. The secret of power is love. *Amor vincit omnia:* "Love conquers all." It may take time, and it may work invisibly, but it works infallibly.

"Creator"—why did God create? He needed nothing, being perfect and eternal. There is only one possible motive: altruistic love, sheer generosity, the desire to share His goodness and glory with others.

"Heaven and earth"—it follows that Heaven and earth, the whole creation, is a song of love because Love is the singer.

Do you see the pattern? Each article in the Creed, each *word* of the Creed, is about God's love. Rather than going through every other word in the Creed, I will assume that the pump has been primed and let you the reader finish the meditation. That would have more educational value than having someone else do it for you. All you have to do is to think deeply about the meaning of the words, and you will find God's love. You don't have to stretch the point. You don't even have to *connect* each article with love, as if love were something extraneous. You just have to look, and you will see love lurking there at the center each time.

The same is true, of course, for the Commandments. They are ways of loving. Everyone knows that Jesus made it perfectly clear that "on these two commandments depend the whole law and the prophets"—to love God with our whole heart, soul, mind, and strength and to love our neighbor as ourselves. It is not just that the Commandment to love is the most important one. It is really the only one. "Love, and do what you will", wrote Augustine dangerously but accurately. It is dangerous because the saying seems to invite the misinterpretation that "doing what you will" could be anything at all. But it is accurate nonetheless because if we do love God, then we will love His will and His law. We will keep His Commandments, but out of love and not just fear or even duty.

Each Commandment makes sense only when you see it in the light of love. Take the first, for example: "You shall have no other gods before me." Why? Because God is an egotist? No, because God is a lover. What lover wants half the heart of his beloved? Also God is a realist. He knows that false gods simply cannot make us happy, however many times we are deceived into believing and acting as if they could. Love, of course, seeks the beloved's happiness. It is God's love of us, not self-love, that is behind His jealousy.

The one Commandment that may seem not to conform to the pattern—*love* does not murder, *love* does not steal, *love* does not bear false witness against neighbor—is: "Thou shalt not commit adultery." It seems that it is precisely love that does commit adultery. But it is not true love, not unadulterated love. True love respects marriages and will not lay them waste.

Each of the Commandments is specific and clear. They show us how to act out of love in different situations. We must love only the beloved and not graven images. Love honors the name of the beloved and does not take it in vain. Love takes time, a sabbath, a sabbatical, or a honeymoon with the beloved. Love honors the authors of its being, the father and mother whose love gave birth. Love does not defraud, deceive, debunk, debar, devour, or dehumanize. Love is the fulfillment of the law.

Finally, everything we are commanded to pray for in the world's most perfect prayer—the only one straight from the lips of God Incarnate in direct answer to the request, "Teach us to pray" (Lk 11:1)—is also love.

We call God "our Father" because we believe in His fatherly love and care.

We want His name hallowed and loved and praised, because we love Him and want others to do the same.

We want His kingdom to come because His kingdom is the kingdom of love.

We want His will to be done, even in preference to our own—we will the abolition of our own will when it is out of alignment with His—because we know His will is pure love. Ours is not.

If *this* is done on earth as it is in Heaven, then we will approach heaven on earth, the annihilation of lovelessness.

We ask for our daily bread because we know His love wants to give it. Love longs to fulfill the needs of the beloved.

We ask to be forgiven as we forgive because love forgives, "It is not irritable or resentful" (1 Cor 13:5).

We ask to be delivered from temptations against love and from the evil that comes when love leaves, because we know "the one thing necessary".

Finally, we praise His kingdom, His power, and His glory because they are nothing but the reign of love.

"Why do you speak of nothing else?" "Because there is nothing else." John the Beloved Disciple knew the point of it all.

3

Defining the Most Important Thing

Definitions are not dull. *Not* having definitions is dull because then confusion reigns and everything is mixed up together like the garbage in a trash compactor.

A definition of love is especially necessary because love, as we have seen, is the point of everything. If we do not know what this love is that is the point of everything, then we do *not* know the point of everything. We only know the word. If we are to put all our eggs in love's basket, what could be more practical, more essential, than to know it is the right basket and not another?

False definitions and false ideas about love have devastating consequences in life. Broken homes, broken hearts, broken societies, broken treaties, our broken world—all result from broken definitions of love, from mistakes about what cement to use to bond these precious and precarious relationships together. A definition alone will not cure the breakage, of course. But without one there is little hope. You need more than a road map to get home, but you need a road map too. And when you are lost—as our civilization is—there is little hope of finding your way without one. A pharmacist needs more than accurate labels, but without them it is unlikely that patients will get the medicines they really need.

There are all sorts of counterfeits on the market, all sorts of false loves, false concepts of love, and false promises about love. The more important a thing is, the more counterfeits there are. There are no counterfeit paper clips but plenty of counterfeit religions. The devil concentrates his strategy on the most important areas of the battlefield.

To define the most important thing in the world, we should use the best language available for our definition. English is a poor language for this. Although it has an enormous number of words, it lacks the subtle distinctions you find in Greek. For instance, Greek has four different words for "know" and four different words for "love". The ancient Greeks hated vagueness and loved precision.

Back to the Greek Definitions of Love

The word the New Testament uses for love, *agape*, is hardly used at all in classical Greek precisely because it was so imprecise. It was a word meaning "love" in general. The other three Greek words for love—*eros* (desire), *storge* (affection), and *philia* (friendship)—were specific words. Thus they were used much more frequently by the people who prized specificity.

When the radically new reality that was Christ the God-Man and His love came into the world, Christians needed a new word for this new kind of love. It was not any one of the three kinds of love already in general use in the language. So the early Christians took the unused word *agape* out of the closet of disuse and gave it a new meaning. Instead of meaning just vaguely or generically "some kind of love", as it had meant before, it now meant the shatteringly new and unmistakable kind of love seen in Christ and Christians.

That this new love was unmistakable and not just love in general or any one of the old forms of love is clear from John 13:35. Jesus says, "By this all men [unbelievers] will know that you are my disciples, if you have love for one another."

In other words, this new form of love will be so different from any of the old forms that it will be unmistakable even to unbelievers. "They'll know we are Christians by our love." That is a test just as essential as sound doctrine in identifying Christians. That is the force that won the world, softened hard Roman hearts, and woke up a tired old society to exclaim: "See how they love one another!" And what about us? What if someone asked, "If you were put on trial for the crime of being a Christian and a practitioner of Christian love, would there be enough evidence to convict you?" What would the answer be?

Agape is a unique form of love. It is not *eros* (desire). Even when desire is not sexual, not physical, and not selfish in an ethical sense, it is always selfish in a psychological sense. The clearest case of *eros*, of course, is sexual desire. But an artist's love of beauty is also *eros*. The artist's love is not a physical need like hunger, but it is a need. It is not selfish as the desire for pleasure or power or money is selfish. Yet, though it may not be sexual, physical, or selfish, it is a need, a desire. It comes from our appetites. It is not a choice. I undergo it rather than freely create it. It is like a wave that washes over me or carries me. But *agape* is free. It is not a feeling, it is a choice.

Agape is not *storge* (affection) for similar reasons. Affection is a spontaneous feeling of fondness for someone or something. It's that feeling of tenderness that wells up inside when you are shopping and the cute baby in the grocery cart next to yours smiles. Or *storge* can be an emotional attachment for someone or something that develops over time. It might be triggered by seeing an old friend or finding a prized keepsake.

But *agape* is (1) not a feeling or an emotional attachment, though it may be accompanied by these things; and it is (2) directed to all, to "neighbor"—that is, to any neighbor. *Storge* is based on a spontaneous feeling or emotional attachment to only some people and things, while *agape*, like an ocean current, runs far deeper than the emotional surface to any and all neighbors in need, whatever we may feel or not feel for them.

Finally, *agape* is not *philia* (friendship) either. *Agape* does have one important feature in common with friendship: freedom. Unlike *eros* and *storge, agape* and *philia* are specifically human, free choices rather than animal instincts or feelings.

But unlike friendship, *agape* need not be reciprocated. Jesus loved His enemies, even His crucifiers, and prayed to His Father to forgive them. That is love, but it is not friendship.

Another difference is that friendship is selective. No one can be friends with everybody. But *agape* does go out to everybody—not to everybody in general but to everybody in particular, to our actual, concrete "neighbor", one person at a time.

God's Love Is More Than a Feeling

We need to focus on exactly what *agape* is if we are to contrast it not only with the other three legitimate loves but also with some popular illegitimate ideas about love, some misunderstandings. The first and most common error is to think that all love is a feeling. Therefore, if *agape* is not a feeling, then it is not love. It is no insult to feelings to note that *agape* is more than a feeling. Many people automatically resent any hierarchy, any insistence that A is higher than B. They think that insults B. But it does not. Are cats lessened by the fact that humans are greater than cats? Is man lessened by the greatness of God? Many think so. But in fact man is exalted if God is great, for then he can be God's image and not just clever dust in the wind, a quirk of some blind evolutionary process.

Feelings come to us; *agape* comes from us. Feelings are passive and receptive. *Agape* is active and creative. Feelings are instinctive, *agape* is chosen. We are not responsible for our feelings, for we cannot help how we feel. But we are responsible for our *agape* or lack of it because our choice to love comes not from wind, weather, digestion, good vibrations, heredity, or environment, but from our own heart, the center of our being. We fall in love, but we do not fall in *agape*. We rise in *agape*.

Feelings cannot be commanded. Only a fool would command you to feel a certain way. But God commands us to love. Jesus had many different feelings for many different people: Peter, John, Mary Magdalen, His mother, Judas, Pilate, and the Pharisees. But He loved them all.

How is love possible without feeling? How can you love someone if you do not like them? Easily. We do it to ourselves continually. We do not always have a tender, loving feeling about ourselves. Sometimes we feel foolish, stupid, asinine, or wicked. But we can still love ourselves and seek our own good. We can even dislike ourselves precisely *because* we love ourselves. We can berate ourselves only because we care about our goodness and are impatient with our badness.

God is *agape*, and *agape* is not feeling; therefore God is not feeling. That does not make God cold and distant, less loving, less fiery, less dynamic. Just the opposite: God is Love itself, while feeling is only the dribs and drabs of love received passively. God cannot fall in love, not because He is less loving than we are but because he is more. He cannot fall in love for the same reason water can not get wet: it *is* wet. God *is* love, and Love itself cannot receive love as a passivity. It can only spread it as an activity. God is love-in-eternal-action.

Wise old Father Zossima in Fyodor Dostoyevski's classic *The Brothers Karamazov* teaches that "love in action is a harsh and dreadful thing compared with love in dreams". Feelings are like dreams: fun, easy, passive, and spontaneous. *Agape* is hard and precious like a diamond.

Jesus Never Once Told Us to Love Humanity

This brings up a second popular misunderstanding, closely related to the first. It is easy to have love for humanity, but it is hard to have it for one's neighbor. For the mass of humanity is not here on my doorstep, my neighbor is. Humanity never surprises you, never disappoints you, never bugs you. Humanity is as safe as a picture in a museum. It is just that: a mental picture in the museum of the mind.

Jesus never once told us to love humanity. If preachers tell you that he did, they are serving up their own recipe instead of Jesus'. The only Jesus we know, the Jesus of the Gospels, told us to love *as he did;* that is, to touch and serve the specific individuals we meet. Jesus did not come to earth for the sake of humanity. He came for you and for me.

Love Is Not Only Kindness

A third related misunderstanding of love is to confuse it with kindness. Kindness is one of the usual attributes of love but not its essence. Kindness is the desire to relieve or prevent another's suffering. But love is the willing of another's good. Both are unselfish, but love aims higher and farther.

It is painfully obvious that God is not mere kindness, for He does not relieve all our sufferings immediately, though He has the power to do just that. Even Jesus, who went around healing, left many unhealed. This very fact—that the God who is omnipotent and could at any moment miraculously erase all the sufferings of the world nevertheless deliberately chose to tolerate so much suffering in the world—is the most common of all arguments used by unbelievers against believing in a good God. The number one argument for atheism stems from this confusion between love and kindness.

The more we love someone, the more our love goes beyond kindness. We are only kind to our pets. Therefore, we consent that our pets be killed to put them out of their misery when they are suffering badly. There is greatly increasing pressure throughout the Western world to legalize active euthanasia, to treat each other as we treat our pets, to seek no higher good than pleasure and freedom from pain. This is a great insult to human dignity. It stems from the confusion between love and kindness as well as the confusion between people and pets, men and animals. Animals are not moral agents. They are innocent; they are not sinners. But they cannot be saints either. St. Francis did not treat animals like people or people like animals.

We are only kind to strangers but more demanding to those we love. If a stranger informed you that he was a thief or a prostitute or a drug addict, you would probably try to reason with him in a kind and gentle way, like a professional. But if your son or daughter told you that, you would not act like a professional, but like an amateur. An *amateur* means literally a lover. Professionals do not do much shouting and screaming and hugging and kissing and crying. Amateurs do. It is the cost of loving those you really care about.

Grandfathers are kind. Fathers are loving. Grandfathers say, "Run along and have a good time." Fathers say, "But don't do this, and don't do that." Grandfathers are compassionate, fathers are passionate. God is never once called our Grandfather in Heaven, much as we may prefer that to the inconveniently demanding and intimate *Father.* The most frequently heard saying in our lives today is precisely the philosophy of the grandfather: "Have a nice day." Many Catholic priests even "sanctify" this philosophy by ending the Mass with it, though the Mass is supposed to be the worship of the Father, not the Grandfather.

A fourth misunderstanding of love is more theological in origin, but its results are felt on the human and practical level. It is the confusion between "God is love" and "Love is God". The worship of love instead of the worship of God makes two deadly mistakes. First, it uses the word "God" as only another word for love, so that God is thought of more as a concept or ideal than as a person. Second, it divinizes the love we already know rather than showing us a love we do not know, a new kind of love.

To understand this last point, consider the following little lesson in logic. "A *is* B" does not mean the same thing as "A *equals* B", for "A equals B" is reversible. But "A is B" is not. If A=B, then B=A, but if A *is* B, that does not mean that B *is* A. "That house *is* wood" does not mean "Wood *is* that house". "An angel is spirit" does not mean the same as "spirit is an angel". When we say "A *is* B," we begin with a subject, A, that we assume our hearer already knows. Then we add a new predicate to it, B, that he does not yet know. "Mother is sick" means: "You know Mother. Well, let me tell you something I think you do not know about her. She is sick."

So "God is love" means: "Let me tell you something new about the God you already know. This God is essentially love; He is love through and through." But "Love is God" means: "Let me tell you something about the love you already know, your own natural, human love: that is God. That is ultimate reality. Seek no further for God. You have already gone as far as anyone can ever go." In other words, "God is love" is the most profound thing we have ever heard. But "Love is God" is idolatry and deadly nonsense.

A fifth misunderstanding is the idea that you can be in love with love. No, you cannot, any more than you can have faith in faith, or hope in hope, or see sight. Love is an act, a force, an energy. But a *person*, a lover or a beloved, is more than that. A person is the most real and most valuable thing there is because a person is the image of God, who is ultimate reality and ultimate value. In fact, God's essential name, "I Am", is the name for a person.

If someone says they are in love with love, their love is not *agape* but a feeling. You can have a feeling for a feeling. You can desire that an emotional state continue. But the object of *agape* is not *agape* but a person.

The old English word for this love was *charity*. What a pity that word can no longer be used without misunderstanding or wrong connotations. Charity now means to most people simply money given to beggars or to the United Way fund. Even when it does not mean money, it connotes something self-conscious, self-regarding, and artificial. It leaves a bad taste in our mouth. No one wants to be the object of another's charity. No one wants to be a "charity case". It means being on the welfare rolls either literally or figuratively.

But *agape* does not have that self-conscious connotation. *Agape* is self-forgetful. Its right hand does not know what its left hand does (Mt 6:3). It gives, yes. But it emancipates rather than enslaving its recipient, and it forgets rather than displaying its giver. Charity is self-conscious thing-giving; *agape* is unself-conscious self-giving.

So the word *charity* will no longer do, nor will the word *love*, because of all the misunderstandings and confusions attached to it. So it seems necessary to insist on the Greek word *agape*, even at the risk of sounding scholarly or even snobbish, to avoid confusion about the most important thing in the world.

Agape *and the Other Two Greatest Things in the World*

Agape is closely tied to faith and hope, the other two greatest things in the world. For the source of *agape* is God and God's grace, which is the gift of God's own life in our souls. That gift is received by faith, grows by hope, and flowers by love. Love is faith's flower, hope is its stem. Grace comes into us by faith, like water through the roots of a tree. It rises in us by hope, like sap rising through the trunk of the tree. And it matures in us by *agape* as fruit matures on a tree's branches, fruit for the neighbor's eating. The three greatest things in the world—the three "theological virtues", faith, hope, and *agape*—are one reality with three parts like a tree.

To change the image, faith is like an anchor. That is why it must be "conservative", stuck fast. Anchors, like roots, are supposed to stick fast so they will hold. Faith must be faithful and steadfast.

Hope is like a compass or a navigator. It gives us direction. It takes its bearings from the stars. That is why it must be our head in the clouds, idealistic, progressive, and forward-looking. Did you ever see a navigator looking backwards?

Agape is like the sail spread to take the wind. It takes us on our journey over the sea of life. That is why it must be liberal, open, and generous.

Agape *Is Never Second, Always First*

Where does *agape* come from? The source of the *agape* we give to our neighbor is the *agape* we have first received from God: "We love because he first loved us" (1 Jn 4:19). When we come to God we find that God has sought us out first. As an anonymous hymn says, "I sought the Lord and afterward I knew / He moved my soul to seek Him, seeking me; / It was not I that found, O Savior true; / No, I was found by Thee." That is why Augustine has God saying to him in his *Confessions*, "Take heart, child; you would not be seeking Me unless I had already found you."

Agape is not second. It is not a response. *Agape* has first place. It is creative, like the act of creating the universe in the beginning. Our *agape* is a participation in God's creativity. *Agape* harkens back to the creation of the universe. It calls us to join in God's creative play.

The clearest way *agape* differs from all other loves is this. Other loves come second. They perceive and respond to some already existing value in the object loved. But *agape* comes first: it *creates* value in its object. Other loves presuppose justice, desert, and deservedness. They are attracted by something, whether physical or spiritual. But *agape* goes beyond justice itself. *Agape* is its own norm and standard.

If the last statement seems shocking or exaggerated, consider this. *Agape* cannot be based on justice as a reason for loving because reasons are always given from above downward, from some prior premise or principle. But there is nothing above or prior to love, for God is love.

That is why the *agape*-lover can answer the question *"How* do I love thee?" only by saying "Let me count the ways." He simply cannot answer the question: "*Why* do I love thee?" Why does God love me? Do I deserve it? No. Then why? Because He is God, that's all. Because that's the way He is. He loves me because He is He, not because I am I. The sun does not shine on the earth for the same reason stones fall to the earth. No earthly gravity draws down the sun's light (though it affects its path once the light is given). The sun shines on the earth not because the earth is the earth but because the sun is the sun.

When he was about five, my son once asked me, "Daddy, why do you love me?" I began to give the wrong answers, the answers I thought he was fishing for. "Because you're such a great kid. You're good and smart and strong." Seeing his disappointment, I decided to be honest and simple instead. "But the real reason I love you is because you're mine." I got a smile of relief and a hug. *Agape* had relieved his performance anxiety. He needed to know that he was loved not because he performed well, not because he merited love. He needed to know that being loved depended on the lover, not on the beloved, like our being loved by God.

A student once asked me in class: "Why does God love me so much?" That one really stumped me. I replied a little frivolously, "Come back a year from now and maybe I'll have the answer." But this student was not frivolous but dead serious. One year later there she was. She really wanted an answer! I finally explained to her that this one thing, at least, could not be explained.

Agape *Is the Foundation of Civilization*

The practical importance of this point, that *agape* does not follow reason and justice but is prior to it, concerns the very survival of civilization. No civilization can survive without justice to persons. But justice to persons is founded on the value of persons, and the value of persons cannot be seen without *agape*. Sigmund Freud is a good example. In *Civilization and Its Discontents*, he argues against altruistic love as the meaning of life and the key to happiness by saying simply, "But not all men are worthy of love." No, indeed they are not. *Agape* is quite defenseless against this objection. The love we are talking about goes beyond reason, and a rationalist like Freud just does not see it. We who take *agape* for granted because of our Christian education should realize its precariousness. There is simply no effective rational answer to the challenge: "But give me a reason why I should love someone who does not deserve it." Love is the highest thing. There can be no higher reason to justify it.

Therefore, if the question of the foundation of social justice to persons is pushed far enough, society must choose between two ways. Western civilization is precisely at this crossroads today. We must either abandon the concept that lies at the basis of our civilization—the concept that persons are ends rather than means, that persons are not just useful things with a practical value that can be calculated—or else we must base justice on this unprovable and unexplainable concept of the intrinsic value of persons. We do not usually realize how rational totalitarian dictatorship is. All the great totalitarian movements in this century have taken precisely the low but rational road by treating persons calculatedly and coldly as things fit to be used for some higher purpose. Will we resolutely take the high and more-than-rational road? The answer is far from clear.

We can no longer just muddle along without raising this dangerous question. The burning issue of abortion forces us to raise it. So does euthanasia. The so-called "quality of life ethic" is deep down more dangerous than nuclear war, for it destroys the very soul of our civilization, not just bodies. It says a human person's value is finite and calculable, that it varies with health, intelligence, and social utility. That is exactly what Hitler believed.

Though *agape* comes from God, it resides in our free will as human beings. Its home is not the body or the feelings, or even the intellect, but the will. True, the intellect has to work with it. But it is not the intellect that loves, any more than it is the light in the operating room that performs the surgery. *Agape* may be aided by seeing, accompanied by feeling, and accomplished by doing, but it is essentially an act of choosing, an act of free will.

If God *is* love, then God must be that which loves, an "I will." God is not just being or the Force or Cosmic Consciousness, but a willer with a will. This is the distinctively biblical concept of God, which is missing in most Oriental religions.

Three other words for the source or agent of love in Scripture are "heart" (the center or core of the person), "spirit", and "I" (as in "I AM WHO AM"). All three mean the self. The source of *agape* is not any function of the self but the self itself, that mysterious and non-objectifiable personal center that is the root and source of all our functions. *Who* is it that thinks and feels? *Whose* body and soul is this? Who am I? "Know thyself."

I sense, *I* think, *I* know, *I* feel, *I* desire, *I* long—there is an "I" behind everything *I* do, inner or outer, spiritual or physical. This *I* is God's image in me. Like God, it is hidden (Is 45:15). For like God, it is the subject rather than the object, the thinker rather than the thought, the feeler rather than the felt, the doer rather than the deed. "Know thyself", then, is the insolvable puzzle—the mystery that cannot be reduced to a problem. The self or I is the thing we are but cannot know, the thing that is not a thing.

The most intimate and central act of the I is willing. I can distance myself from my thoughts, hold them captive as an object and criticize them. I can do the same with my feelings. But not with my willing—at least not my present willing—for the very act of holding something before my consciousness *is* an act of willing.

I am not wholly free or responsible for my thoughts and feelings, which partly come to me from my heredity and my environment. But I am completely free and responsible for my will's choices, which come *from* me. I *am* not what I think or feel, but I *am* what I will. I can distance myself from my thought. I can even distance myself from my feeling, for I can feel angry and yet refuse to be identified with that feeling. But I cannot distance myself from my willing. I cannot will and refuse at the same time because refusal is willing.

That is why it is not important whether temptations come to me, but it is important whether I consent to them. "Not what goes into the mouth defiles a man, but what comes out of the mouth, this defiles a man" (Mt 15:11). This is true not only of the mouth or the body, but also the soul. What comes *into* my soul is not necessarily what I will, but what comes *out* of my soul is precisely what I will.

The Greek philosophers did not clearly recognize this personal center. They were intellectualists; they thought the deepest thing in us was the mind. Thus Plato taught that whenever we really know the good, we do it. He thought that all evil is ultimately ignorance and curable by education. Aristotle too identified reason with the true self, that which distinguishes us from animals. He defined man as "a rational animal". But Scripture goes deeper. When asked how people could understand His teachings, Jesus replied, "My teaching is not mine, but his who sent me; *if any man's will is to do his [the Father's] will, he shall know* whether the teaching is from God" (Jn 7:16–17, emphasis added).

The will leads us to wisdom. The heart leads the head. Therefore Solomon says, "Keep your heart with all vigilance; for from it flow the springs of life" (Prov 4:23). In the natural sciences the head must lead. But when knowing *persons*—ourselves, others, or God—the heart must lead the head. "Deep calls to deep" (Ps 42:7), I to I. Thus Augustine declares that his *Confessions* cannot be understood by those who "do not have their ear to my heart, where I am what I am".

"Know thyself" was the first and greatest commandment for the Greeks. It was inscribed on every temple of Apollo. We can distinguish at least five levels of profundity in attempting to answer that fundamental question: What is the self? What am I? What is the human person? Only the key of love unlocks the deepest answer.

Answer no. 1: I am the social self. I am simply a social function, an ingredient in society. Society is the absolute. This old tribal view is coming back into modern consciousness. Many of my students use "Society" (always with a capital S, like "Science") exactly where theists would use "God", as the ultimate authority. De Tocqueville, Kierkegaard, Nietzsche, Ortega y Gasset, Huxley, Orwell, and Riesman all warned of this: "photocopied" souls, standardized selves, mass conformity, "the lonely crowd".

Answer no. 2: I am the individual physical self. I am the thing that eats, diets, jogs, exercises, and dies. I am what I eat. This old pagan materialistic notion is also undergoing a great comeback in the modern yuppie world.

Answer no. 3: I am the feeling self. I am a mass of self-actualization, loneliness, positive and negative energy, different strokes, complexes, libidinous urges, or other vibrations of the psyche. This is another very popular view in the modern world. It is a little deeper and closer to the heights reached by classical paganism, which is the next deeper view.

Answer no. 4: I am the rational self. Unlike the animals, which include all the above answers, I can know truth. I stand in a light for which the animals have no receptor: the light of understanding, meaning, and intrinsic value. "Reason" meant this to the ancients: something immeasurably greater than what "reason" means to moderns, greater than calculation, cleverness, or logical correctness. To the ancients, it meant a divine attribute: wisdom.

Answer no. 5: I am the will, heart, soul, spirit, self, or I. I am that which chooses, commits, decides, and loves.

Why is the fifth answer the truest one? The will is central because love is central. Not the intellect. Not quite. Plato is half right: evil does indeed come from ignorance, but not *only* from ignorance, for then it would be excusable. In fact, ignorance first comes from evil. We will, we choose, we create the moral ignorance in our souls, the ignorance that Plato saw as a prerequisite to doing evil. We voluntarily turn off the light of truth. For instance, we shut out the divine truth and justice of "thou shalt not steal" before we sin by stealing. The ignorance of the thief—by which he thinks that filling his pockets with stolen money will make him happier than filling his soul with proper virtue—is indeed, as Plato saw, a prerequisite for his act of theft. But that ignorance in turn has as *its* prerequisite the will's choice to turn the thief's attention away from the truth of the moral law. He wills to look instead at the pleasures he thinks will derive from his loot. His ignor*ance* come from his ignor*ing*.

Agape *Moves Us toward Heaven*

Augustine says all evil comes from disordered love, for it is love that moves me where I go. Love is my gravity: *Amor meus, pondus meum*, "My love is my weight." I go where my love moves me. That is why all persons are either going toward God and Heaven or away from God and toward Hell.

My identity and my eternal destiny are determined by my love. For what I love becomes my end, and my end is my destiny. Augustine's great masterpiece *The City of God*, the world's first philosophy of history, is the story of these two cities, these two spiritual organisms, these two invisible bodies intertwined through history, beginning with Cain and Abel. Like a cancer that has infiltrated a healthy human body but lives a different life, the City of the World, though visibly mixed with the City of God, is as different from it as cancer cells from healthy cells.

Love is why all are members either of the City of God or of the City of the World. "Two cities have been formed by two loves: the earthly by the love of self, even to the contempt of God; the heavenly by the love of God, even to contempt of self. The former, in a word, glories in itself, the latter in the Lord" (Augustine, *The City of God*, XIV, 28).

This story of these two cities is the fundamental drama of history, the story behind the headlines. It is really the same drama as that of Augustine's other masterpiece, *The Confessions*, in which we see the two cities in his own life, his own soul. It is a drama of two loves, the old story of "the eternal triangle": whom will I marry? God, my true beloved? Or some idol, and thus ultimately myself? That is the fundamental option, the fundamental question of every human life. That is what decides Heaven or Hell. Compared with this even clarity of thought and feeling happy are trivial.

Agape *Seeks the True Good of the Beloved*

What does *agape* aim at? What is its goal? *Agape* differs from other loves not only in its origin but also in its end. Not only does it come from God and the will, but it also seeks the end of objective goodness, not subjective happiness.

Personal fulfillment or self-actualization is not the aim of *agape*. *Agape* is unselfconscious, not self-regarding. It seeks the good of the beloved, not of the lover. And it thus attains the good of the lover in the only way possible. As Jesus tells us, only the one who loses his self can find it (see Jn 12:24–25).

Agape also looks at the *true*, *real*, and *objective* good of the beloved rather than at subjective feelings, whether of the lover or of the beloved. It looks at needs rather than wants. This is how *agape* differs from compassion. Compassion wills the subjective good of the beloved—good feelings, contentment, happiness, and freedom from suffering. Compassion is kindness. But *agape* wills the objective good of the beloved. This usually includes the subjective good of the beloved, and thus love usually includes kindness or compassion. But it goes beyond them. Thus it wills or tolerates suffering when suffering is necessary for the beloved's true, objective good. That is why loving parents discipline their children, and why God does not wipe away all tears from our eyes until Heaven (Rev 21:4).

When We Really Love, We Give Ourselves Away

Finally, there is a mind-boggling mystery about *agape* which we must look into. Somehow when we love we really give ourselves away. We do not just give of our time or our work or our possessions. No, we give ourselves. How can this be? How can I put myself in my own hands and hand it over to you?

The way to illuminate a paradox is by another paradox. Here it is. I can do this unthinkable thing because when I do it, another unthinkable thing happens: I find myself in the very act of losing myself. That paradox is well known— "Lose your self to find it"—but it remains just as paradoxical no matter how familiar it becomes. I begin to be when I give my being away. I get a new and real self only when I give up my old self, like a snake shedding its skin. The self I thought I was is only the skin.

There is even more to the paradox: nothing else is really mine. My health, my works, my possessions, my intelligence, my life itself—these are not what they seem. They are all loans, hostages to fortune. They are shifting rainbows, insubstantial and ephemeral. I discover that when I stand face to face with God in prayer or when I stand face to face with death in fear. I discover that I am nothing.

The saints sometimes say this: I am nothing. Thus God said to Thérèse of Lisieux: "I am HE WHO IS and you are SHE WHO IS NOT." The closer you get to God the more you see this. Those who scorn God think they are Number One. Those who have conventional ideas of God think they are "good people". Those who have a merely intellectual orthodoxy know they are real but finite creatures made in God's image but flawed by sin. Those who begin to pray find that compared with God they are dust motes in the sun. And finally, saints say they are nothing—or else in the Apostle Paul's words, "the foremost of sinners" (1 Tim 1:15). Sinners think they are saints and saints think they are sinners.

Who is right? How shall we evaluate these diverse testimonies about who we are, these five different levels of answers to the fundamental question "Know thyself?" Unless God is the father of lies—which is the ultimate blasphemy, for we know who *that* is—the saints are right. Unless the closer you get to God the closer you get to deception, the five classes are ranks in a hierarchy of truth. And the saints have the most truth.

Surely they are right; for our very existence is not ours, but sheer gift and loan. Think clearly and squarely for just one moment about the fact that you were created out of nothing. If a sculptor gives a block of marble the gift of a new shape, that shape is his gift to the marble, but the marble's existence is not. But nothing is our own because we were made *out of nothing*. Our very existence is a gift from God to no one, for we were not there to receive the gift before He created us. There is no receiver of the gift of existence distinct from the gift itself. The gift *is* the receiver. We *are* God's gifts.

So nothing can be ours by right, by nature, or by necessity. But one thing is mine by my free choice: the self I give away in love. This is the thing even God cannot do for me. It really is *my* choice. God can love, but He cannot compel my free love. If it is compelled, it is not free. If it is free, it is not compelled.

So everything I usually think of as my own is not ultimately mine. But everything I think of as given away and no longer mine but yours, is really mine. C. S. Lewis, when asked which of the many books in his library he thought he would have in Heaven, replied, "Only the ones I gave away on earth and never got back."

It is not a flippant answer but a profoundly accurate one. Lewis' books are symbols of our very selves. The self is like a baseball. Throw it back to the divine pitcher who pitched it to you in the first place, and the game of love goes on. Hold it, and the game is over. That is the difference between Heaven and Hell.

4

Deeper into the Definition of Love: Scripture's Classic on *Agape*, 1 Corinthians 13

We now turn from my attempt to define and describe *agape* to what divine revelation says about it. We begin a journey of exploration into 1 Corinthians 13: the greatest essay ever written about the greatest thing in the world.

It is divided into three parts. The first three verses are about the all-excelling *value* of *agape*. The next three verses are a fifteen-point *description* of *agape*. And the last six verses are about the *destiny* of *agape*.

This famous chapter is placed between chapters 12 and 14 like a piece of meat in a sandwich. The meat is well known but not the bread, the surrounding context, chapters 12 and 14. These chapters, like the rest of Paul's letter, deal with some of the problems the church in Corinth was having, especially one that has become an issue again in the Church for the first time in centuries: the charismatic gift of tongues.

This gift was widespread among the Corinthian Christians and that seemed to make them feel somewhat superior, even arrogant. It was a perfect opportunity for Paul to come down hard on these first-century charismatics, as many present-day Christians want to come down hard on our contemporary charismatics. But Paul does not censure the gift itself, only its loveless use. This affords him entrance into a topic infinitely more important than the gift of tongues: *agape*.

Paul's attitude toward tongues is balanced. The gift itself, he says, is authentic, supernatural, and good. Further, it is for everyone in the Church. Paul says that he himself speaks in tongues more than anyone else. But the gift must be regulated by good sense, order, unity, and above all by *agape*.

It is Paul's constant habit in his epistles to use the local and temporary issues that arose in the congregations to whom he wrote as an opportunity to teach universal and perennial principles. First Corinthians 13 is the most famous example of this method. If a principle is truly universal and unchangeable, then it must apply to all places and times. Thus the universal and unchangeable principles of *agape* must apply to the problem of tongues in Corinth and the problem of tongues in America today and the problem of denominationalism and the problem of liberation theology and every other problem in the world.

Love is not one of the charismatic gifts like tongues or prophecy or miraculous healing. It is not called a "gift" but "a more excellent way" (12:31). That is, it is the way to use all the gifts. It is the thing that makes the difference to everything else. Even good things, like the supernatural gift of tongues, or martyrdom—"if I should give my body to be burned"—are not good without *agape*. *Agape* is the catalyst that makes value appear in anything. It is what makes a child's crude, hand-drawn birthday card infinitely more valuable than a grudging gift of a million dollars.

Agape is one of the "fruits of the Spirit" (Gal 5:22). Tongues are one of the "gifts of the Spirit" (1 Cor 12:4–11). What is the difference between a gift and a fruit? First, gifts are immediate. For instance, one receives the gift of tongues suddenly and all at once, like a Christmas present. But the fruits of the

Spirit, like physical fruits, take time to ripen. We do not attain love or joy or peace instantly.

Second, the gifts are more external. They are given from without. The recipient of a gift is essentially passive. But the fruits are more internal. Though they too come from God, from without, they are received less passively and more actively through our choice and work. Like a plant, we must do the growing through our own free cooperation. We must train ourselves in the fruits as habits. Even fruit growers cannot make fruits grow. The fruits grow themselves.

Third, the gifts are primarily for the community, for the edification of the Church, and for a testimony to the world. But the fruits are primarily for the individual, for personal holiness. They are of supreme importance because they perfect the most important things in the world, the things that will still be alive after all the galaxies have died: persons created in God's image.

The gifts of the Spirit are listed in 1 Corinthians 12:4–11. The gift of tongues is well down the list. The fruits of the Spirit are listed in Galatians 5:22–23. Love heads the list, then joy and peace.

The Value of Agape

> If I speak in the tongues of men and of angels, but have not love, I am a noisy gong or a clanging cymbal. And if I have prophetic powers, and understand all mysteries and all knowledge, and if I have all faith, so as to remove mountains, but have not love, I am nothing. If I give away all I have, and if I deliver my body to be burned, but have not love, I gain nothing (1 Cor 13:1–3).

In these first three verses Paul compares the infinite value of *agape* with the finite value of five other extremely valuable things. Even if I have these other things in their fullness, precious as they are—and every one of them is more precious than all the gold in the world—if I do not have *agape*, I have nothing at all. *Agape* is not 51 percent or even 99 percent with these other things making up the rest. *Agape* is 100 percent.

The reason why they cannot be compared with *agape* as percentages of the total is that *agape* is not *outside* these other things. It is not an addition to anything valuable. It is the heart and soul of all value. All other things of value are the hands or head or feet or eyes of *agape*. *Agape* is the heart of value.

The five things Paul mentions are placed in a hierarchy, from the lowest to the highest. The first is the gift of tongues. If I speak with the tongues (languages) of men—as the disciples did at Pentecost, a miraculous phenomenon that has recurred through the Christian centuries—but lack *agape*, my speech is mere noise. I am like the clanging of a cymbal or a garbage can lid. Even if I speak in the tongues of angels—a heavenly language rather than an earthly one—even this is nothing without *agape*. The angels themselves are great only because of their love. Paul is neither saying that we *do* speak in angelic languages nor that we do not. He is only emphasizing that even if we do, without *agape* even that would be worthless. What transforms worthless noise into worthwhile communication is *agape*. And there is certainly a lot of worthless noise in our lives today!

To appreciate this point we must understand the high value that the Greeks, the audience to whom Paul is writing, put on language. They saw it as the thing that most clearly distinguished man from beast. They defined man as "the animal who has language" (*zoon echon logon*). The Greek word for language, or speech is *logos*. It is a word with a much deeper and wider meaning than any of the words we can use to translate it into English. For *logos* means not only (1) *word* but also (2) *thought* and (3) the object of thought, or *truth:* meaning, intelligibility, and form. There is a deep and close connection among these three meanings. John 1:1 could well have been translated, "In the beginning was the Thought", or "In the beginning was the Truth." Jesus is called not only the Truth of God and the Thought of God but also "the Word of God", the speech of God, the tongue of God. Language is so important that Jesus Himself is called God's language.

But God's language is love. Therefore even a supernatural language, if loveless, is not heavenly but hellish. The gift of tongues is often counterfeited by Satanists, by the way, as it was by ancient worshippers of demon spirits. Tongues are not a guarantee of Heaven, but *agape* is.

Paul next compares *agape* with something much more important than tongues. In fact, it is the most important of all the charismatic gifts listed in 14:1–5. This is the gift of prophecy. A prophet is a mouth or mouthpiece for God. He speaks God's word. He does not merely praise God in human words. He speaks not for man to God, but for God to man. How precious are the very thoughts of God which a true prophet brings us!

Yet even a prophet can speak without *agape*, as Balaam's donkey did in Numbers 22, or as Moses did when he struck the rock in anger (Num 20). Jesus said that the greatest of all the prophets under the old dispensation was John the Baptist (Lk 7:28). Therefore, John must have prophesied with *agape*, for he was certainly not "nothing". Even a prophet is that without *agape*, according to Paul. Yet John's style was harsh rather than kind. Therefore, we cannot tell whether or not a prophet is speaking with *agape* just by his style. *Agape* calls for kindness on some occasions and harshness on others. To give kindness when harshness is needed is no more *agape* than to give harshness when kindness is needed, for *agape* means going by the needs of the other, not the inclinations of the self. It was Jesus' *agape* for the Pharisees that made Him harsh to them. It was shock therapy, their last hope, the thing they desperately needed.

The third thing Paul compares with *agape* is understanding. This is the very highest kind of understanding, the understanding of all "mysteries". These are the great hidden truths of God like the Trinity, or the mystery Paul refers to in Ephesians, God's secret plan to save the whole world through Christ. Understanding these things is a far greater thing than prophecy, for these mysteries are the "things into which angels long to look" (1 Pet 1:12). Our modern American anti-intellectual, anti-contemplative, practical, and worldly age appreciates the value of contemplation and of supernatural mysteries about as much as a medieval mystic would appreciate the value of a stock market investment tip.

Yet even this great thing is nothing without *agape. Agape* is greater than understanding because it is the essence of Heaven, our final end and beatitude, while understanding is only its accompaniment. The accompaniment divorced from the essence is like the bass notes without the melody. When Jesus defines eternal life as "knowing" God (Jn 17:3), He does not mean understanding truths about God but loving God as a person, as Adam "knew" Eve (Gen 4:1).

Fourth, Paul says love is even greater than faith. This is even more remarkable, for faith is even greater than understanding in this life. The whole Christian life begins in faith, progresses in faith, and culminates in faith. Only in Heaven will knowledge replace faith when we no longer see "through a glass, darkly" but face to face. Without faith no one can please God (Heb 11:6). Without faith no one can be saved (Jn 3:18). Jesus was constantly exhorting people to faith and bemoaning their lack of faith. For faith is the golden key that unlocks all the doors of our life to God's presence and power. There was nothing that Jesus sought more than faith, except love. Faith is the necessary beginning of the Christian life, but love is its consummation. Faith exists for the sake of love, as the root exists for the sake of the fruit, as the beginning exists for the sake of the end. Even faith, without the works of love, is dead (Jas 2:26).

But even the works of love are no substitute for love itself. And the fifth and last thing Paul mentions that is nothing without *agape* is *agape's* own works. For instance, I can give away all that I have and even let my body be burned in suffering as a martyr, but it is all for naught without love. You can be a martyr without love: an angry, hateful martyr. A terrorist suicide bomber is not an apostle of love.

Even good deeds without love are nothing, for God does not want deeds first of all but hearts. He owns the cattle on a thousand hills (Ps 50:10). He does not need anything from us. God could perform all the deeds He desires, but even He cannot give Himself one thing: our free love. That is the thing that is most precious of all to Him, and He has put it in our charge!

What a wonderful simplification it is to know that there is "only one thing necessary" (Lk 10:42). Correctly understood, the popular songs are absolutely right: "All you need is love." "If we only have love. . . ." But most people who mouth these lines mean by love sex or sentiment rather than *agape*.

Agape is "the one thing necessary" because it will lead to all the other things we need.

1. It will lead to the true and acceptable worship of God. In fact, it *is* the true and acceptable worship of God, who delights not in burnt offerings but in contrite hearts (Ps 51:15–17).

2. It will lead to discernment of God's will. Only if our will is set to do the will of the Father can we understand the Son and His teaching (Jn 7:17). We do not understand *things* by loving them. The love of things and of the money that can buy things blinds our understanding. But we understand persons only by loving them. And God is a person, not a thing. So if you *want* to know God's will with all your heart, you *will*.

3. *Agape* will also lead to holiness and obedience and sanctity. For if we love God, we will want to obey Him. In fact, only the power of love enables us to obey Him, to surrender our will to His.

4. *Agape* will also lead to justice, social morality, and true love of neighbor, for *agape* is "love in action", not "love in dreams". Love will produce its own appropriate deeds. It is not that the subjective motive alone is enough, but that good motives and good works are inseparable. Good trees produce good fruit (Mt 7:17).

5. *Agape* will even lead to heavenly understanding. Those who love God most will understand Him most in Heaven. In fact, that is true even on earth. Simple lovers know what nuanced scholars do not. Simple saints are wiser than sophisticated theologians—though it is possible to be both, as was Aquinas.

6. *Agape* will lead to the one thing everyone seeks in and through whatever they seek: happiness. Not a temporary, subjective, shallow, or false happiness but one that is lasting and true. It is not just happiness but blessedness.

7. Finally, *agape* offers us the peace the world cannot give (Jn 14:27). Dante reveals the hiding place of peace: "In His will, our peace." The twentieth-century British poet T. S. Eliot calls that the most profound line in all of literature. This "yes" to God's will, this word of love, is the whole

secret of worship, understanding, sanctity, justice, contemplation, happiness, and peace. This is the one "pearl of great price" (Mt 13:46, KJV) that is worth giving up everything else in the world to get. And it is free.

Listen to poor families that have become rich talk about their past. They usually say much the same thing: the best years, deep down, were the poor years because then they had more love. Listen to Mother Teresa's sisters in Calcutta. They have an incredible joy amid their incredible poverty because they have an incredible love. The exchange of even a little love for a lot of worldly goods is the most foolish exchange we can possibly make. "For what will it profit a man, if he gains the whole world and forfeits his life?" (Mt 16:26). Yet we make that exchange over and over again.

Agape is astonishingly simple. That is what makes it difficult. It is not too complex for us, we are too complex for it. We must learn to become like little children if we are to find the Kingdom of Heaven (Mt 18:3). For God is like a little child: utterly single-minded and pure of heart. That's how He can govern the universe: right from the center of it all. And that's how we are called to govern our lives.

The Nature of Agape

> Love is patient and kind; love is not jealous or boastful; it is not arrogant or rude. Love does not insist on its own way; it is not irritable or resentful; it does not rejoice at wrong, but rejoices in the right. Love bears all things, believes all things, hopes all things, endures all things.

Here at last, in 1 Corinthians 13:4–6, is what *agape is*. Paul has first told us *agape*'s surpassing *value* so that we would approach this description of its nature with thirst rather than just curiosity. He told us that *agape* is the one thing that gives value to all things. Even the greatest things in the world—supernatural gifts, prophecy, understanding, faith, and the works of love themselves—are nothing without *agape* beating at their heart. *Agape* is the *summum bonum*, the greatest good, "the chief end of man", the meaning of life, the alternative to emptiness and "vanity of vanities", the answer to Ecclesiastes and the modern world.

So what *is agape*? What is the kind of love that fulfills these extreme claims? It is (1) not just *eros*, sexual desire or activity or satisfaction, modernity's most popular substitute. It is (2) not just *storge* or feeling, not even the great and good feelings of instinctive affection, not even mother-love. It is (3) not even the more spiritual love of friendship (*philia*). Friendship is sharing, but sharing another's emptiness is not yet fullness, only compensation for emptiness. *Agape* alone is fullness. *Agape* alone is big enough to fill the hole in our heart that is bigger than the galaxies.

We need a description of *agape* so that we can identify it and distinguish it from its many counterfeits and from its three little sister loves. The description is needed not just for theoretical but for practical reasons. In fact, it is a matter of life or death. These verses are a road map in the desert of our lives to the only water that will never turn out to be a mirage. The description of *agape* is similar in purpose to the Church's creeds that describe Christ. They distinguish the genuine article from alternatives. They draw the borders. They are "truth in advertising".

Paul does not give us a philosophical definition, an abstract and logical setting-out of genius and specific difference. Instead of thus *defining agape*, he *describes* it by giving us fifteen concrete and identifiable attributes of it. They tell us what it is by telling us what it *does*. This is what scientists call an "operational definition"—the most practical kind.

All fifteen features are things we deeply desire. But only *agape* can supply them. *Agape* is the skeleton key that opens these fifteen doors. Take the first, for instance, patience. How can we become patient? By praying, "God, give me patience and do it right now!"? No, despite our good intentions, despite our sincerity, despite our need, we find ourselves continually losing patience even with those we love most. The natural loves, valuable as they are, are not enough. They are like a garden (to use C. S. Lewis' metaphor from *The Four Loves*), but they need a gardener with rake and hoe. That is the role of *agape;* it cultivates and perfects the other loves. When we have *agape* toward someone, it becomes not only possible but natural to have patience toward him, for "*agape* is patient".

Just try being patient without *agape*. It simply will not work. It works only as long as you *feel* patient. So then you try substituting hard "will power" for soft feelings. "I'll be patient with that so-and-so if it kills me." And it almost does. You discover two things: that your will is ridiculously weak and that even when you succeed in repressing your impatience, it is still there. You have buried it alive; it is not dead. Your love is false and forced and formal. Patience has to come from the heart, not from either undulating feelings or from iron resolution.

Agape is the catalyst not only for other virtues, like patience, but also for other loves like affection or liking. When we have *agape*, we find that we can begin liking the people we used to dislike. Once you truly love someone, you no longer rely on liking them, and the surprising result is that you end up liking them more and not less. If this seems unrealistic, reflect that it is exactly what you do to yourself. You love yourself; you will your good, even when you do not like yourself. And the more you love yourself, the more you end up liking yourself. All you have to do is to apply this love of self to love of neighbor, exactly as Jesus said: love your neighbor as you love yourself.

Agape is even a catalyst for the perfection of erotic love. Selfish sex is not even good sex in the erotic sense. Lust spoils sex just as addiction spoils alcohol. Winos cannot appreciate wine, which God invented "to gladden the heart of man" (Ps 104:15). Just so, sex addicts cannot appreciate sex, which God also invented for that same reason among others. They lack the self-forgetfulness needed for true joy. The only way to total sex is total love of the beloved. And this means giving your whole self, body and soul, to the one beloved. That is the reason for monogamous, lifelong, faithful, noncontracepted marriage. Polygamy, divorce, adultery, and contraception all pollute Love's Yes with some No. In sex, too, losing yourself is the way to find it.

"Agape *Does Not Insist on Its Own Way*"

If any one of the fifteen attributes Paul lists is to be selected as the one closest to the heart of *agape*, it would be that "*agape* does not insist on its own way".

We are all born into this world with original sin. The simplest way to see this is to watch a toddler. He acts kind and patient when he feels like it. But he is also arrogant, rude, jealous, boastful, irritable, or resentful when he feels like it. In other words, he always insists on his own way. When kindness is his way, he is kind. When not, look out! "My will be done" is inscribed on our soul as our spiritual heredity. It goes even deeper than Freud's "pleasure principle"—a fact Kierkegaard understood when he wrote in his *Journals:* "If I had a servant who, when I asked for a glass of water, brought me the world's costliest wines blended in a chalice, I would dismiss him to teach him that true pleasure consists not in what I enjoy but in having my own way." Our innate dream is Frank Sinatra's line: "I did it my way." We think that is Heaven. In fact, it is the song they sing in Hell.

Agape is the antidote to this fatal spiritual disease we are all born with. "Love is the fulfillment of the law" because "love does not insist on its own way" but on God's way. It says "Thy will be done" instead of "My will be done." And it means it.

Is this possible? That a self should be unselfish, that a will should say, "Not my will"—isn't this a contradiction and an impossibility? No, it is not a contradiction but a paradox, and not an impossibility but a miracle.

Buddha did not understand this miracle, though he understood the disease it cures better perhaps than any non-Christian ever did. His "First Noble Truth" of *dukkha* (suffering) is the profound insight into the depth of our alienation from ourselves through our insistence on our own way. His "Second Noble Truth" sees that "the cause of *dukkha* is *tanha*," "grasping" or selfish desire. He sees that our problems are not in our world first of all, or in our society, or even in our behavior, but in our being. The problem is not in some peripheral aspect of our being that a good psychiatrist could cure, either. It is in our very will, our very center. He sees that we cannot be cured except by radical surgery. Few other thinkers ever dared to see and admit that terrible truth. However, Buddha's only surgery is spiritual euthanasia, killing the patient (ego, self, will, I) to cure the disease (egotism, selfishness, self-will, "mine-ness"). His therapy is to eliminate all desire, all will, and all sense of self.

But there's good news. There's no need to go to Doctor Buddha for euthanasia. The patient can be cured even of this innate disease. The leopard *can* change his spots (see Jer 13:23). For *agape* dissolves the apparently indissoluble glue that bonds egotism to ego, selfishness to self. It kills the cancer of selfishness and creates underneath it a new heart (Ps 51:10), a new God-given self which "does not insist on its own way".

Thus Jesus' prognosis of the human condition is the greatest of all paradoxes: "Whoever would save his life will lose it, and whoever loses his life for my sake will find it" (Mt 16:25). Buddha saw the first part of this paradox but not the second. He saw the symptoms and the disease but not the prognosis and the healing. The modern West does not even see the disease. Instead, we justify our innate selfishness by making it pleasant and gentle and respectable. Hug yourself. Be your own best friend. We're O.K. Look out for Number One.

A poll revealed that of all the scientists in America, those in psychology include the smallest percentage of religious believers. Astrophysics and cell biology were among the highest—probably because they study divine order rather than human disorder. Right at the center of life we have an irrevocable conflict of philosophies: Jesus versus the vast majority of modern psychologists on how to save your soul and even on whether you *have* a soul. Unless Jesus is simply wrong, if you follow this vast crowd of false prophets who dominate our age, you will quite possibly lose your soul. (Of course, there are good and even great psychologists, but they are not the reigning orthodoxy.)

But if you let your natural self-will die and be replaced by *agape*, by the love that does not insist on its own way, you will be reborn. Give up what you think is your self and you will find what God has designed as your real self. Give up your own way and you will find yourself getting your own deepest way, the happiness you always longed for but somehow could never attain without *agape*.

The modern West affirms both self and selfishness; the traditional Orient denies both. The common premises of both philosophies, modern Western and ancient Eastern, is that the two must always go together. Jesus comes with a sword, a surgeon's scalpel, and divides selfishness from self, sin from sinner, as a cancer must be separated from its healthy host. We are to love sinners passionately, as He did and as the Orient does not. But we are to hate sin passionately, as He did and as the modern West does not.

Jesus does not merely give us *advice* about *agape*. He gives us *agape*. He exchanges selves with us: we are put in Him, and He is put in us. He *is* the Love that "does not insist on its own way". First Corinthians 13 is a description of *Christ*. His *love* can be in us only because *He* is in us. We attain *agape* not by trying a little harder but by faith, by believing and thus receiving (Jn 1:12), by letting Him in, letting Him invade us, possess us, haunt us.

Love Bears, Believes, Hopes, and Endures All Things

Finally, what does Paul mean by saying that *agape* bears, believes, hopes, and endures all things?

Jesus does this. He is *agape* incarnate. He bears all things like Atlas bearing the world on his shoulders. He does not only bear His own Cross, He bears the crosses of the whole world. He bears His Cross to the world, and He bears the world to His Cross. The Cross is His surgeon's knife. The patient and the doctor meet on Calvary's operating table.

Agape believes all things and hopes all things because Jesus' faith and hope are as infinite as His charity. Jesus always believes in us more than we do in ourselves. Look how God believed in Job even when Job hardly believed in God any more. He is the ocean that buoys us up and will not let us sink.

And *agape* endures all things because Jesus endures all things. Everything suffered by each cell of His body (us!) is suffered by Him. This is no clever symbolism or myth or exaggerated way of saying that He sympathizes with us. It is literally true. Jesus Christ experiences everything that you experience, the least of your joys and the greatest of your sorrows. You never suffer alone or laugh alone or pray alone or even blink alone. "Lo, I am with you always" (Mt 28:20). Did you think that was empty rhetoric? He never spoke empty rhetoric. "Surely he has borne our griefs and carried our sorrows" (Is 53:4). Did you think that meant mere sympathizing? "Truly, I say to you, as you did it to one of the least of these my brethren, you did it to me" (Mt 25:40). Did you think that was only an edifying myth? Whatever we make our brothers and sisters endure, we make Him endure, because He is *agape* incarnate; and *agape* endures all things.

C. S. Lewis ends the greatest sermon I have ever read outside the Bible, "The Weight of Glory", with the insight that "next to the Blessed Sacrament itself, your neighbor is the holiest object presented to your senses", for in both Christ is truly hidden. Though He is hidden, *agape* has x-ray vision, and here is what it sees:

> It is a serious thing to live in a society of possible gods and goddesses, to remember that the dullest and most uninteresting person you can talk to may one day be a creature which, if you saw it now, you would be strongly tempted to worship, or else a horror and a corruption such as you now meet, if at all, only in a nightmare. All day long we are, in some degree, helping each other to one or other of these destinations. . . . There are no *ordinary* people. You have never talked to a mere mortal. Nations, cultures, arts, civilizations—these are mortal, and their life is to ours as the life of a gnat. But it is immortals whom we joke with, work with, marry, snub, and exploit—immortal horrors or everlasting splendours.[1]

[1] C. S. Lewis, *The Weight of Glory and Other Addresses* (New York: Macmillan Publishing, 1980), pp. 18–19.

And that leads us right to Paul's capstone, the eternal *destiny* of *agape*.

The Destiny of Agape

> Love never ends; as for prophecies, they will pass away; as for tongues, they will cease; as for knowledge, it will pass away. For our knowledge is imperfect and our prophecy is imperfect; but when the perfect comes, the imperfect will pass away. When I was a child, I spoke like a child, I thought like a child, I reasoned like a child; when I became a man, I gave up childish ways. For now we see in a mirror dimly, but then face to face. Now I know in part; then I shall understand fully, even as I have been fully understood. So faith, hope, love abide, these three; but the greatest of these is love (1 Cor 13: 8–13).

The Irish poet William Butler Yeats tells of watching a little girl on a beach in Normandy as the waves washed away her sand castles, thinking of all the many great cultures and civilizations that had been washed away by the waves of time in that place and plaintively wondering, "Will anything last?" The Apostle Paul addresses that question in these last six verses of 1 Corinthians 13. What do we have here in time, if anything, that lasts forever?

Our possessions and the body with which we possess them will not last. "You can't take it with you" as the ancient Egyptians fondly supposed you could, burying their dead pharaohs surrounded by riches.

Not even faith lasts forever, for faith means believing what cannot be seen or what can be seen only "through a glass, darkly", through a misty windowpane. There will be no need for faith in Heaven, for we will then see God face to face. Beholding the face of God will replace faith.

The very stars do not last forever as the ancients mistakenly thought. Buddha knew better. He taught that "whatever is an arising thing, that is also a ceasing thing". He called this universal truth "the pure and spotless eye of the *dharma* (doctrine)". But Buddha did not know one "arising thing" here under the sun that is *not* a "ceasing thing". He did not know the one reality in our lives that will outlast the sun because it comes from beyond the sun: *agape*.

Do you ever wonder why you will never be bored in Heaven? The question is far more serious than it seems. Boredom is modern man's deepest fear. Death was ancient man's deepest fear, and Hell was medieval man's deepest fear. But "vanity of vanities", a sense of emptiness and consequent boredom, is the specifically modern enemy. In fact, there is not even a *word* for generalized boredom in any ancient language! Boredom is at the root of the widespread unconscious drive to destroy all forms, limits, order, law, and reason. It is the dark urge Freud called "the death wish". The dark mind of the dark prophet sometimes sees better in the dark than the children of light (cf. Lk 16:8).

No one can run with hope or passion toward a goal that seems boring. But everything here is eventually boring. Even the atheistic philosopher Jean-Paul Sartre said, "There comes a time when you say even of Shakespeare, even of Beethoven, 'Is that all there is?'" How can we understand anything of Heaven if there is nothing at all on earth to compare it to, nothing heavenly, nothing that never gets boring? Thus either Heaven is boring, or something on earth is not boring, or nothing on earth is like Heaven.

There are two parts to the answer: first, that everything on earth except *agape* is *meant* to be boring; and second, that *agape* is not.

God designed all finite things to be eventually boring because He designed our heart with an infinite hole in its center, a hole that cannot be filled even with the whole enormous but finite universe. There is a Black Hole in our heart analogous to the physical Black Holes in intergalactic space that can suck all the matter in the universe into themselves. This spiritual black hole is the restless heart that will not and cannot rest anywhere except in God, its home.

God designed earthly things for time. Planned obsolescence was part of the design for everything created. (That is why we must let go even of our hold on our own beloved dead.) Every well in the world, however refreshing, runs dry. But our souls thirst for the living water that springs up fresh forever from the throne of God.

Like it or not, we come into this world with predesigned equipment, spiritual as well as physical. And we can never alter or erase that design, no matter how desperately and darkly we try. We are cursed with the knowledge of God. We are spoiled by our knowledge of the Best and can therefore never be wholly satisfied with anything less. Even if we suppress this truth (Rom 1:18), nevertheless "truth will out". "Nothing is hid that shall not be made manifest, nor anything secret that shall not be known and come to light" (Lk 8:17). Freud himself tells us how. Whenever we bury knowledge in our subconscious, it always shoots up somewhere else, cracking its own gravestones.

The deeper and more honestly we look, the closer we approach Ecclesiastes' terrifying truth about this world: "Vanity of vanities, all is vanity." In fact, Pascal says, "Anyone who does not see the vanity of this world must be very vain himself." Unless we know only our hearts' shallows and not their depths, nothing here under the sun can fill our hearts and still our restlessness.

But God can fill us and still us, and God is *agape*, and *agape* is here under the sun. *Agape* is eternal because it is the very stuff of God. That is why it is the only thing in life that never gets boring. Not ever. *Agape* is the only answer to Ecclesiastes. Ecclesiastes says, "I have seen everything" (Eccles 1:14). But he has not. He missed one thing: *agape*.

Even the other loves get boring. Selfish love gets boring because if I love you for me—to fill up my need and my inner emptiness—then I am eventually filled (superficially)—and bored. Or else I am not filled—and frustrated. In neither case can I be happy. There is no possible escape from the dilemma of boredom versus frustration within the framework of egotism. Only the breaking of that framework by *agape* can ever solve the dilemma. Only *agape* can ever make us happy forever.

We have tried everything else, and every one of our billions of experiments with life have failed. Yet, so incredible is our foolishness, we keep trying, hoping that the next wife or husband or job or vacation or drink or drug will bring us the happiness we always longed for, however darkly. That is the deepest reason why the psychiatrists' couches and the divorce courts are filled. That is the one reason they never tell you about in psychology or sociology courses.

We never have found and never will be able to find anything that does not eventually wear out and get boring. But we can *give* what never ends and never bores: *agape*. Heaven will not be boring, not because we will get forever, but because we will give forever. Living forever without giving forever is not Heaven. It is Hell.

As the great line of one of John Denver's songs puts it, "If love never lasts forever, then what's forever for?" What *is* eternity for? For *agape* and nothing else. Eternalize anything else and you spoil it. Even the natural loves eventually spoil. Affection becomes cloying. *Eros* becomes a drug requiring ever-increasing doses of perversions to ward off the boredom. Even friendship finds rocks to founder on, for though its sea is immense, it has shores.

Paul announces the absolute exception when he tells us in three simple but astonishing and revolutionary words: "*Agape* never ends." "Luv" ends, but love never ends. "I shall love you forever" usually means about two months. A billion promises, and only *agape's* are not broken. As C. S. Lewis says in *The Four Loves*, *eros* makes promises but *agape* keeps them.

One day everything will be made of *agape*. All those things that we made of *agape* in this world will last and be in Heaven. But nothing else. The only thing that will not be burned up in the final fire is the one thing that is stronger than the fire of destruction: the fire of creation. For *agape* is the fire of creation. God created sheerly out *of agape*. Just as the only way to control a passion is by a stronger passion, just as the only way to conquer an evil love is by a stronger good love, the only way to endure the final fire is not by any water that tries to put it out, but by the only fire that is stronger still: *agape*. This is the very fire of God's essential being. Only love is stronger than death.

Even the spiritual gifts fail, supernatural as they are. Paul tells us in verse 8: "As for prophecies, they will pass away; as for tongues, they will cease; as for knowledge, it will pass away." (This refers to the charismatic "gift of knowledge", not knowledge itself. Of course, there will be knowledge in Heaven.) The spiritual gifts are for time. *Agape* is for eternity. Even the spiritual gifts are imperfect (v. 9). Everything in this world is.

No, that is wrong, not everything. A messenger from another world, a perfect world, is here in this world. This messenger is the only perfect thing in this world. That's what Paul tells us in verse 10: *agape* is *perfect*. "When the perfect comes, the imperfect will pass away." *Agape's* perfection is a prophet of doom for the imperfect. When the baby is born, the placenta is no longer needed. It drops off or is cut off and dies.

We must die to our spiritual childhood as to our physical childhood. Jesus does not tell us to *remain* little children but to *become* little children, new kinds of children, truly adult children. The Holy Spirit is our spiritual obstetrician; He urges us onward and upward to birth and newness. Christianity is the most progressive, the most forward-looking idea that has ever entered the mind of man. How it ever got the bad press of being stagnant, retrogressive, or conservative in the pejorative sense of the word, I could never figure out. It must be that Satan, like Hitler, knew that the Big Lie will work where the little lie will not.

The knowledge we now have, even by revelation and faith and the spiritual gifts, compared with the knowledge we will have in Heaven, is as a pinhead to a galaxy. For we will then know *even as we are known* (v. 12). That is, known by God. How are we known by God? Completely, perfectly, infallibly. Did you get that incredible point? We will know completely and perfectly and infallibly. We will know ourselves as God knows us. Only in Heaven can the earthly command "Know thyself" be adequately obeyed.

What then remains? In time, three things never die: faith, hope, and love (v. 13). But the greatest one, love, is the only one that remains even after death. Faith and hope bring us through time but leave us at the doorstep of eternity. Only love goes with us inside.

Faith and hope are like the first two stages of a three-stage rocket. They are jettisoned when they have launched the third stage, the payload, the whole point of the whole rocket. This third stage of our spiritual rocket, unlike a physical rocket, is ignited at the same time as the first stages. It travels with them through the space of time, but it is freed from them when the rocket reaches a critical altitude. The altitude is death. At death, we receive our hearts' deepest desire as the heart of the rocket, *our* heart, is launched into the heart of the rising Son.

Christa McAuliffe, a victim of the space shuttle Challenger disaster, was a Christian. That meant that her soul had its own three-stage rocket. Dare now to imagine what Christa felt when the space shuttle's rockets exploded and she suddenly found herself, now out of her body, propelled faster and farther than any man-made rocket could ever go, beyond the earth, beyond the universe itself, into the lap of God! It was not any solid or liquid fuel that brought her that far. It was the fuel of *agape*.

Like homing pigeons flying home, like iron filings drawn irresistably to a magnet, like solar flares falling back to their parent sun from which they had sprung, lovers of God become one with the fire of their Beloved. The twentieth-century British poet Stephen Spender wrote their epitaph: "Born of the sun, they travelled a brief while toward the sun and left the vivid air singed with their honor."

That is what a Christian is. Not to be one is life's only real tragedy.

5

The Theology of *Agape:* God Is Love

This is the most difficult and abstract chapter in the book. Its subject, the mystery of the Trinity in love, is one about which we can hope to understand only the tiniest hints and guesses of the infinite, blinding light of truth that is there. That is why I shall keep this chapter very short and to the point.

Centuries of thoughtful and prayerful meditation on the words of Scripture, especially the text "God is love" (1 Jn 4:8), aided by natural reason—particularly as articulated by the best of the Greek philosophers—has resulted in the following essential theology of God's love. It is one of the Church's deepest treasures.

1. Love is God's essence. Nowhere else does Scripture express God's essence in this way. Scripture says God is just and merciful, but it does not say that God is justice itself or mercy itself. It does say that God *is* Love, not just a lov*er*. Love is God's very essence. Everything else is a manifestation of this essence to us, a relationship between this essence and us. This is the absolute; everything else is relative to it.

2. Love is one with God's personhood and being. The only other Scripture passage where God's essential being is revealed is the passage in which God reveals to Moses His true name: I AM (Ex 3:14). I-ness or personhood is God's essence. So is AM-ness or being. So is Love. These are all somehow one in God's essence.

3. Love requires a lover, a beloved, and the act of loving. Love necessarily means three things: there must be a lover, a beloved, and the act or process of loving. Thus for God to be Love itself—the whole of love, the whole essence of love complete in Himself independent of creatures—He must be somehow all three: lover, loved, and loving. If He were only one, He could be a lover of all that He created, or the beloved of all that He created, but not Love itself.

4. God is three persons in one essence. God is three persons—Father, Son, and Holy Spirit—but one essence, one being, one God. The one God *is* the three persons. The three persons *are* the one God.

5. The three persons know and love each other. The Father knows and loves the Son. The Son knows and loves the Father. The Holy Spirit eternally proceeds from this love. He *is* this love between Father and Son, as the Son *is* the Father's knowledge ("Word") of Himself.

6. The processes of love in God are without beginning. The Son does not have a birthday in Heaven, and the Spirit does not wait to proceed until *after* the Father and Son have exchanged their love. The Father eternally generates the Son and the Spirit eternally proceeds, not as temporal processes with beginnings and endings but as eternal, timeless activities.

7. The Son is with the Father as our thoughts are with us. He is both (a) God himself and (b) together with (in relationship with) God (Jn 1:1). Reflections of this divine mystery are not wholly absent from our human experience since we are made in the image and likeness of this God. The Son is also called the Word (*Logos*) or thought of God. Our thoughts, our inner words, are also both (a) ourselves and at the same time (b) *with* us. They are in relation to ourselves, in dialogue with ourselves, so to speak. We can carry on a conversation with our thoughts as if they were characters in a drama we were writing. They sometimes seem to tremble on the brink of getting an independent life of their own, especially in the writings of the great creative artists like Shakespeare. Macbeth or Shylock or Hotspur are almost real to us. God is the next step up in creativity, so to speak. God's thought is actually real, not almost real, like Shakespeare's thoughts.

8. The Father loves the Son in knowing and generating Him. The Father's thought—His one total, omniscient, all-inclusive thought—is a *He*, a person: the Son. The Father's eternal act of generating (begetting) the Son is at the same time the act of knowing Him and loving Him. In the very act of generating the Son by knowing Him—like generating a thought—the Father loves Him. In fact, He loves the Son into being. The Son has being only because the Father loves Him and wills Him. (Knowing, even in us, doesn't just happen: we do it; we will it.) But this is not a temporal process, either in its cause (the Father) or its effect (the Son): both are eternal. In the act of creating the universe, the cause (God) is eternal but the effect (the universe) is temporal. The Son is eternal and without beginning. He does not come into being at any time. He does not come *after* the Father.

The most important and practical point is not the elusive one about eternity, but the point that in God, the three absolutes are one: being, knowing, and loving. The more God-like we are, the more they will be one for us, too.

9. The Son loves the Father in eternity and in time. The Son reciprocates this perfect knowledge and love of the Father back to Him, both in Heaven (in eternity) and on earth (in time, during the Incarnation). When the Son comes to earth and time, He says He comes not to do His own will but His Father's will (Jn 6:38). His Father's will is His very life-food (Jn 4:34). It is to be ours too. Again, the dogma has crucial practical application.

10. The Holy Spirit is the love between Father and Son. Just as the Father's *Logos* is so real that it is a distinctly real person, so the Father and Son's mutual love is so real that it is a distinctly real person, the Spirit. And the Spirit is third not in *rank*, for all are equal, nor in *time*, for all are eternal, but in *order*—as the hypotenuse is the third side of a right-angled triangle.

11. Having babies is a remote but real human analogy to this mystery. Because we are made in God's image, our love images His. Thus a mother and a father love a baby into existence by giving themselves to each other. This is an image of the Father and the Son loving each other so fully that the Holy Spirit proceeds from Their union. The common feature is that a third person comes from the love of two other persons. The difference is that with a human family the process has a before-and-after sequence in time. And it is a material, biological process. In God, it is eternal and spiritual. But the likeness is as real as the difference.

12. This is the ultimate origin of the holiness of sex, reproduction, and the family. Consciously or more often unconsciously, this Trinitarian origin and model is the ultimate reason the Church has traditionally looked on sex, reproduction, and the family as sacred. From the world's point of view, the Church is hung up on sex because she fears it. But the truth is rather that she cherishes it as reflecting the mystery of the Trinity. She does indeed have fear, but it is an adoring fear, not a servile one. It is sacredness, not scaredness. She sees sex as awe-full, not awful.

The Love of God Has Invaded Our World, and We See with New Eyes

I have laid out the mystery of Trinitarian love and some of its practical applications to our lives in twelve propositions, almost as if it were a scientific formula. Not only might that leave the wrong impression—as if the ultimate mystery of divine love could be encased in formulas that we could clearly and adequately understand—but even worse, it leaves out another *dimension* of the truth. This is one which most of us have tragically lost and need to recover, a dimension that cannot be put into words and sentences, though words and sentences can be used to suggest it.

All premodern societies had this other dimension, even the ones who were very far from having the propositional truth, the Christian content of revelation. Most of the readers of this book need only a little refresher course on the propositional content of the theology of Trinitarian love, which I have tried to provide here. But most of us have a far greater need of recapturing the other dimension I wish to speak of. This other dimension is a vision, a perspective, a habit of seeing rather than a specific thing seen. If we do not have this habit—this vision—then our theology will not sink much deeper than the conscious, rational level.

The thing I speak of can be called myth, imagination, analogy, or sacramentalism. All four words are slippery and ambiguous. Rather than trying to define them, let me give an example. Indeed, let me give the crucial example for our purposes here, for our topic in this chapter is the theology of love and how it applies to our lives. Without this way of thinking, such an application, such a connection between what God is and what we are, is tenuous and strained.

Since God is the Creator and since creation reflects and reveals the Creator, and since God is love, all creation somehow reflects and reveals love. That is a logical argument, but my point here is not to *deduce* the conclusion but to *see* it, to understand it, to stand under it. If God is love, all creation must reflect love. Yet we do not habitually look for these reflections. For instance, we no longer understand, except as a quaint historical curiosity, the idea that sexuality is not just biological. We have lost the idea, implicit in almost all the languages of the world except English—which has no masculine and feminine nouns—that human sexuality is the human version of a universal principle. When other languages call the sun "he" and the moon "she", they are not simply projecting the human reality out onto nature, but seeing something that is really there. One version of this is the famous Chinese *yin* and *yang*. Another is the Indian marriage ceremony in which the groom says to his bride, "I am heaven, you are earth." She responds, "I am earth, you are heaven."

Many readers will find such ideas utterly unintelligible and perhaps suspiciously pagan. Why should a Christian take seriously the fact, for instance, that all the pagans peopled the sky with male gods and the earth with female goddesses? This sounds very strange to our ears.

The basic point, freed from polytheism, is not *only* pagan, any more than anything universally human is pagan. It is

Christian too. Dante was a great Christian poet, with all of a great poet's power of imagination. However, the famous last line of his *Divine Comedy* is not poetic fancy but sober and profound fact: it is indeed "love that moves the sun and all the stars".

This is what we no longer spontaneously see. When we look up at the night sky, we do not see—as did the ancients—the glory of God. We have to be reminded of it, perhaps by a memorized quotation from Scripture. When we see the stars we do not hear "the music of the spheres", but only silence. When we think of gravity, we do not think of it as the body of love or the material expression of love, as Dante did. We do not see God's love at work in the very structure of matter.

Let's try to do just that. Have you ever wondered *why* there is gravity? Science explains that every particle of matter attracts every other particle according to fixed laws, proportionate to mass and distance. But science does not explain *why*. Why does that funny little electron in a hydrogen atom keep doggedly orbiting around its positively charged nucleus rather than zooming off orbit in a straight line? The scientific answer is: because its angular momentum, which tends to move it straight away from the nucleus, is exactly counterbalanced by its electromagnetic attraction to its oppositely charged nucleus. But why? Why is it attracted to its nucleus? Why do negative and positive charges attract? Do you not see a real connection between this and love? Juliet loves Romeo because he is Romeo. And the electron loves (unconsciously, of course) its proton because it is a proton.

We can see the same principle at work on every level: gravity and electromagnetism on the inorganic level, a plant's attraction to the sun and to water and nutrients in the soil on the plant level, instinct on the animal level, and love on the human level. And within the human sphere there is also a hierarchy, beginning with the sexual desire (*eros*) and affection (*storge*) that we share with the animals, up to the friendship (*philia*) and charity (*agape*) that we share with the angels. The universe is a hierarchy of love. This is not a myth. This is the splendid and glorious truth. Look! How can you miss it? It is all around us.

Science's reductionistic method fails to see cosmic love. Modern science requires the use of the simplest possible explanation. This is the principle called Occam's Razor. The modern mind always tends to reduce the greater to the lesser rather than seeing the lesser as reflecting the greater. It thinks of human love as only complex animal instinct, or even complex electrochemical attraction, rather than thinking of these subhuman attractions as love on a lesser level. Premodern thought saw lust as confused love. Modern thought sees love as rationalized lust. This is reductionism.

Christianity is anti-reductionistic. Christians cannot buy into reductionism, for they know that God is first. They know that the universe resembles God rather than vice versa, that God made man in His image rather than vice versa. They know that the best comes first, not last. They know that animal love is a latecomer and imitator of perfect, eternal, divine love rather than vice versa. Evolution can never be the *ultimate* explanation for a Christian. Nor for that matter, for a good philosopher: how can more come from less? It violates the elementary principle of causality.

An example of the influence of modern reductionism on the Christian mind is this: there are two relationships between Creator and creature. But modern Christians usually remember only one of them. First, God loves everything. Second, everything loves God. The second is as true as the first. Acorns grow into oak trees because they are in love with God. That is, they seek (unconsciously) their own perfection, which is a participation in some of God's perfection. An oak tree is more perfect, more Godlike, than an acorn. An acorn is not satisfied to be an acorn, because it wants (unconsciously, of course) to be more like God. God is the magnet that draws all the iron filings that are creatures closer to Himself. *That is why everything moves*. It is seeking its own perfection, which is a reflection of God's perfection. Everything moves out of love of God.

The point can be put in the sober, commonsense terms of Aristotle's philosophy. Any complete explanation of anything or any event, says Aristotle, must include four factors or "causes".

The "material cause" tells what it is *made of*. For instance, we say that the house is made of wood or that the sonnet is made up of fourteen lines of iambic pentameter or that Aristotle was made of flesh and bones.

The "formal cause" tells what it is *made into*, what its form, nature, essence, or definition is. This house is a private home or residence. This sonnet is a rhymed poem. Aristotle was a rational animal.

The "efficient cause" tells what it has been *made by*. The house was made by a carpenter. The sonnet was written by Shakespeare. Aristotle was the product of sexual generation from his two parents.

The "final cause" tells what it is *made for*; its purpose, goal, good, or end. The house is to shelter a family and its goods. The sonnet is to express love to the poet's lady fair. And Aristotle, like every man, existed to pursue and attain happiness through knowledge of truth and love of goodness.

Of these four causes, the fourth is the most important because it is the reason for all the others; it is "the cause of causes". Carpenters build houses only because families knowingly seek shelter. Acorns grow only because they unknowingly seek their natural end, to become oak trees.

Now God is not only the first *efficient cause* of the universe, its ultimate origin. He is also the last *final cause* of the universe, its ultimate end. "I am the Alpha and the Omega" (Rev 1:8), the beginning and the end, Jesus tells us. Thus everything in the universe is and lives and moves and has its being not only *from* God, but also *toward* God. Augustine's great line is true of everything in nature as well as man: "Thou hast made us for [*ad*, 'toward'] Thyself, and [therefore] our hearts are restless until they rest in Thee."

The whole universe is a vast circulatory system. The blood of being is pumped by the divine Heart through the arteries of creation (efficient causality) and returns through the veins of love (final causality).

Everything loves God in its way. Not only did God love everything into *existence* by creation, He also loves everything into *perfection* by being the universal Beloved. Not only does God love everything, but everything loves God. Only man can move contrary to this principle of nature through freely choosing evil. Every *thing* loves God, but not every *one* loves God.

But all this is only analogy, you say? True: acorns, electrons, tomcats, men, and angels do not love God in the same way. But, then, neither does God love acorns, electrons, tomcats, men, and angels in the same way. That is why they are different; because God loved these differences into existence. If we do not balk at the latter analogy, why balk at the former? In both cases we have real similarity, real analogy, neither simple sameness nor simple difference, but real likeness.

Thus the theology of love gives us a whole new worldview. We have moved from the eternal relationships among the persons of the Trinity to tomcats because the apparently abstract and theoretical theology of the inner life of the Trinity as love turns out to have the most radical and revolutionary consequences for our view of everything in the universe and everything in our daily lives. It brings us back to the forgotten wisdom of the myths. It plunges us into a world that really does shout the praises of its Creator. It allows the Heavens really to declare the glory of God (Ps 19:1). That is not just clever poetic artifice. It frees us from the dusty, dirty, smelly little dungeon of a universe that "Enlightenment" thought gave us: a universe in which love and beauty and praise and value are mere subjective fictions invented by the human mind, a universe in which the only things that are objectively real are blind bits of energy randomly bumping into each other.

This theology reinforces our own instincts. Our own deepest instincts are to see love as the highest wisdom and ultimate meaning of life. The theology of divine love, which anchors this instinct in the nature of ultimate reality itself, tells us that our deepest values "go all the way up". It also extends this instinctive wisdom, that sees love as the ultimate meaning of things, into the entire creation. The arms of the Savior on the cross reach up to the Absolute and down to the depths of the human heart and across the whole universe from atoms to archangels. When Jesus threw open his arms on the Cross, he said, in effect: "See? That's how much I love you."

6

The History of God's Love: Scripture as Love Story

As we saw in the last chapter, the love of God is a timeless truth, an eternal fact about God, the essence of God, the life of the Trinity, what God *is*. But once God creates a world of time, this timeless truth becomes also a temporal truth. This love becomes a love *story*. Like white light refracted through a prism and split into many colors, God's eternal love-nature, expressed through the prism of time, becomes God's multicolored love story. History is His story.

Love fits itself to the needs of the beloved. We creatures of time need to be addressed in terms we can understand. Therefore, God shows us His love in temporal terms.

There are two forms of this story: the doing and the telling. The doing is the events of history (all of them); the telling is the special selection and interpretation of events that make up the story in Scripture. In this chapter we will look at Scripture as the telling of God's love story.

Scripture claims to be "true" (Rev 22:6). What does Scripture mean by truth?

The three most important and influential cultures of the ancient world—the three whose contributions have lasted throughout all subsequent history—each have a different word and a somewhat different meaning, slant, or angle on truth. These three cultures and languages are all represented at the central meeting point of history, Calvary. On the sign posted over Christ's cross was written the world's charge against Him in Greek, in Latin, and in Hebrew. Let's look at the Greek, Latin, and Hebrew concepts of truth.

The Greek word for truth, *aletheia*, contains the word *Lethe*, the river of forgetfulness in Greek mythology. *Aletheia* means literally "not-forgetfulness". It connotes the idea that truth is a knowledge that is innate in us, and what we need to do is remember it. It also connotes the idea that this process is a struggle, that forgetfulness is our first and natural condition, that truth is found by digging, by questioning, by a kind of intellectual warfare against forgetfulness. Both these connotations are dramatically present in the Socratic dialogues and in the philosophy of Plato. It is a notion of truth perfectly fit for the philosopher: a voyage of intellectual discovery of a treasure hidden by forgetting, as by sleep, and revealed by remembering, as by awakening, by emerging from the cave of ignorance into the enlightenment of knowledge, as in the famous parable of the cave at the beginning of Book Seven of Plato's *Republic*.

The Latin word for truth is a more moral and practical word. It is *veritas*, and it connotes rightness, lawfulness, and properness in thought: thought's *virtue*. The intellect is seen as coming under the more basic categories of the will and morality. Truth is rightness in thought, as justice is rightness in deed.

The Hebrew word for truth is more primordial and basic than either the Greek intellectualistic *aletheia* or the Latin moralistic *veritas*. It is *emeth*, and it means "fidelity" or faithfulness. It is a quality not of a *thought*, but of a *person*. It doesn't even point to a *deed* but to the character of the person as revealed in his deeds.

The Greeks ascribed truth to thoughts, the Romans to deeds, the Jews to persons: first to God, then to human beings when they conformed to God by believing His promises and obeying His will as revealed in His laws. Hebrew truth is personal—not in the modern sense of being subjective and relative like a matter of personal opinion, but in the sense of utter reliability in a person. It is akin to the holding-together-ness of a person, like a bucket that "holds water" because the bottom will never fall out. That is what Scripture means when it says that God is "faithful and sure (true)" (Is 25:1).

Now the *eternal* truth of God's nature—which is love—is expressed, revealed, and played out like a movie onto the screen of time in the *historical* truth of God's fidelity to His people and to His promises. This is the center of love, tough-love, the hard core of love. Feelings and sentiments are the soft flesh of love, but *emeth* is its skeleton, its bone structure. In God essential truth equals essential love.

Our response to God's truth, God's faithfulness, must be our own truthfulness, our own faithfulness. Thus there is an identity between truth and faith. Faith is truth in relationship. In the intellectual sphere, faith and truth are not identical because faith means believing an idea to be true and truth means that an idea corresponds to reality. Faith is the relation between mind and idea, and truth is the relation between idea and objective reality. But if we take both concepts out of the intellectual sphere and put them into the sphere of persons and personal character, they meet: a true person is a faithful person.

Trace the word "true" through Scripture with a concordance. You will be surprised how often the word refers to something that *comes* true in time, especially a promise made by God. Count the promises in Scripture. You will find hundreds of them, and all are guaranteed to come true. This is a dramatic, dynamic conception of truth. Truth is not something static but something that happens in history. It is something you can *see*!

But before you see it, you must believe it. Instead of "seeing is believing", Scripture teaches that believing is seeing. For instance, when Jesus assures Martha in John 11 that He is "the resurrection and the life" and Martha believes Him, He then goes on to raise her brother Lazarus from the dead. He assures her, "Did I not tell you that if you would believe, you would see?" (Jn 11:40). Jesus accepts even doubting Thomas' way of believing only after he sees, but it is not the best way: "Have you believed because you have seen me Thomas? Blessed are those who have not seen and yet believe" (Jn 20:29).

But all who believe *will* see. Faith is not like bottled water but like rain. Its destiny is not just to be kept and held but to make something visible grow. It is an investment, and it has a payoff. It is a leap, and there is a landing. It is empirically verifiable, though often not until the next life and always after a time-test of faith and patience.

The other great religions of the world center on something other than history: on timeless truth or Nirvana or the eternal oneness of everything with Brahman or the Tao. Only Judaism and Christianity and, to a lesser extent, Islam are *essentially* historical religions. Take away everything historical from any of the other religions of the world and you still have the essence left: the myth, the message, the mysticism, the morality. But take away the historical events that are the foundation of the religions of the Bible, and the whole structure collapses like a skyscraper without a foundation. Christianity is not essentially a set of abstract values but a set of historical facts. "If Christ has not been raised, then our preaching is in vain and your faith is in vain" (1 Cor 15:14).

So Christianity is essentially a story. What kind of story? There are all kinds: detective stories, war stories, romances, psychological dramas, tragedies, comedies, spy stories. What kind of story is history, according to Christianity? Another way of putting the question is: what kind of story *are* we in? That's the question Sam asks Frodo as they journey on their daunting and seemingly hopeless quest into Mordor in J. R. R. Tolkien's epic *The Lord of the Rings*:

> "I wonder what sort of a tale we've fallen into?" [asked Sam]
>
> "I wonder," said Frodo. "But I don't know. And that's the way of a real tale. Take any one that you're fond of. You may know, or guess, what kind of a tale it is, happy-ending or sad-ending, but the people in it don't know. . . ."[1]

But the Bible lets us know. It is the only book that can tell us what kind of a tale we're in with assurance, because it is the only book that has been written not just by the human characters inside the story but also by the divine author of the story. Its perspective is double, that of the characters and that of the author, or that of the human authors and that of the divine author. Christ is the Word of God in person. The Bible is the Word of God in writing. Both are the Word of God in the words of men. Both have a human nature and a divine nature.

And we are still in this story! The divinely guaranteed interpretation of the story is complete, and the canon of Scripture is closed. But the story itself is carried on by ourselves.

[1] J. R. R. Tolkien, *The Lord of the Rings* Part II *The Two Towers* (New York: Ballantine Books, 1965), pp. 407–8.

> "Why, to think of it, we're in the same tale still! It's going on. Don't the great tales never end?" [asked Sam]
>
> "No, they never end as tales," said Frodo. "But the people in them come, and go when their part's ended. Our part will end later—or sooner." [2]

What kind of story are we in? Our story includes all kinds of stories, of course. But what is the point, the unity of the whole complex thing? The Bible's answer is that *we are in a love story*. We are notes in a love song. Every movement of every molecule is a vibration of the universal lyre of love.

That is why the Song of Songs has been the favorite book of the Bible for so many saints: it lifts the curtain a little and lets us in on the divine secret behind the scenes, the point of the play we are in. All the other stuff in the play—all the war and suffering and death and law and punishment and spy stuff, all the stuff that seems so different from a love story—is part of the love story. It is *in* the love story as darkness is in a picture or a novel or a musical composition. The contrasting strokes set off the main theme, the villain sets off the hero, the dissonant chords set off the higher harmony of the whole.

It is an enormous claim, of course, even an apparently outrageous one. How dare anyone say a little child's painful death is part of a love story? But let us look before we leap either into it in faith or away from it in rebellion. Let us study the whole picture before deciding whether it is a masterpiece worth buying or a forgery that deserves burning.

What Pulls the Story Together?

Let us start at the center and point of it all, the unity in this crazy quilt of diversity. Christians call the Bible the *Word* of

[2] Ibid., p. 408.

God. Why not call it "the *words* of God"? It has millions of words in it. It contains many books and many authors. How is it *one* Word?

The answer can be found in John 5:39–40. Jesus says to the Jews, who possessed the true Word of God in the Old Testament Scriptures but who would not believe in Him:

> You search the scriptures, because you think that in them you have eternal life; and it is they that bear witness to me; yet you refuse to come to me that you may have life.

What irony! The whole point of the Scriptures is to give us eternal life by pointing to the Savior, the Life-giver. Yet many know the words but not the Word, the many signs but not the One signified, the pointing fingers but not the person they all point to. That is like preferring a photo album to a person. Old Testament Scripture is Christ's photo album, and those who refused Him had their noses in the pictures and could not see the person. They were eating the written prescription from the druggist instead of taking the medicine it prescribed. Life Himself was standing before them, and they kept spelling it out "L . . . I . . . F . . . E".

Jesus is the Word pointed to by the words. The Bible is a complex portrait of Jesus. Each word is a line in His face. But to recognize the face you need comprehensive vision, floodlight understanding, not just the spotlight knowledge of each detail. You need to see the whole picture.

The analogy of the portrait works nicely. As a physical entity, a portrait is many things: many molecules, many lines, many colors. But the person that the portrait is or means or signifies is one. That is what makes the portrait one: the portrait gets its unity from the person it portrays, rather than from the molecules that make it up. Similarly, the Bible gets its unity from Jesus, not from the books that make it up.

Scripture is not just the words of God but the Word of God because its unity is Christ the Word of God.

And Christ is love incarnate. He is incarnate *because* He is love. The Incarnation happened only because of love, both His and His Father's love (Jn 3:16). He came out of love, He shows love, teaches love, exemplifies love, lives love, and finally dies for love. He is the point of the Bible and He is pure love; that is why the Bible is a love story.

The Three Parts to Every Story

Like all stories, this one has three parts. It is sometimes said that there are only seven basic plots, but there is really only one. It is this: every story must have three parts: a situation is set up, then upset, and then reset, whether successfully (happy ending) or not (sad ending). There is first a world and characters and a life: the setting. Then there is a problem, an irritant that gets the characters and the plot moving. Finally, the conflict is dealt with and resolved, or at least addressed. Situation, challenge, and response are three stages of every story.

God's story follows these three stages, too. Actually, every story follows these stages *because* God's overall story does and not vice versa. In Christian theology, they are called creation, fall, and redemption. God first sets up the situation, which is essentially a love relationship between Himself and mankind (Adam and Eve). Then the man and woman upset it by the fall, the great divorce against God. Then God resets it with the long history of redemption. And His strategy is cleverer than that of any spy story, leading history to an incredible victory by buying back His human beloved from the clutches of Satan and sin.

All three stages manifest love:

A. Creation manifests love. The God of the Bible, as distinct from the gods of pagan religions, is one, perfect, self-sufficient, and independent. He did not have to create. He has no needs. He is perfect and complete and fulfilled and happy by Himself in eternal joy because He is a Trinity and not just a Unity. Thus He is never lonely.

This doctrine of God's independence apparently removes God from the realm of love. If He does not need us, does He then really love us? Is not the doctrine of God's independence and needlessness a remote, arid, elitist, and snobbish theology?

Exactly the opposite. The doctrine of God's independence and perfection safeguards God's love rather than threatening it. For if God needed me, then creating me was selfish. It was for Him and not just for me, not purely an act of altruistic love. Only if God created for sheer gift, not need, was His act sheer love, total self-giving, and unselfish generosity.

Furthermore, creating me meant loving me from non-existence into existence, and that means loving me absolutely, not for any merit or deservedness on my part. This love must go beyond justice. God created me out of perfect freedom. We are never wholly free but always somewhat limited and constrained by circumstances and conditions outside our control. Therefore we cannot create being from nothing. We can only make and shape and change already existing things. The fact that God created me out of His perfect freedom means that the whole cause of my existence is God's will. God simply willed me (and the whole universe that eventually produced me) into existence. God gave me *being*. What could be more absolute love than that? Nothing forced God or even influenced God to create me except His own free love. He willed me to be absolutely and unqualifiedly. To will the other absolutely—this is absolute love.

The God who created time is not subject to time, as everything in the created universe is. Therefore He knows everything, even the things that to us are not yet. What to us is future is already known to God as present. All is present to God. So God must have foreseen all my sins and rebellions against Him, all the trouble I would cause Him, including the hell of Calvary. Yet He chose to create me. The word *fore*seen is not perfect in this context, for it seems to put God into time. But it helps get across the point.

God knew that I would be like Adam and Peter and Pilate, and even Judas. He knew that my sins would necessitate His crucifixion if His love was to be successful in winning my soul. In the act of creation He saw the Cross. Yet, knowing the infinite price to Himself, He still chose to create me. He loved me despite the nails I put into His own body. He prayed for *me* from the Cross and said "Father, forgive them", (Lk 23:34) even as I crucified Him. What crazy love is this? It is Love itself. It is the love of the Author who chose to create a story with His own hellish agony in it, so that He could create a story with my heavenly joy in it. Creation manifests absolute love.

B. The fall manifests love. This brings us to the second stage of the story, the fall. The connection between the fall and love is freedom. Love does not enslave, but frees, the beloved. God's love gave us free will. With it, we chose sin and we fell. Thus even our fall, our sin, is proof of God's love. Only in freedom can we sin. And only love gives us the freedom to sin. Without that freedom to sin there is also no freedom to love.

We doubt God's love when we see and feel all the sufferings that our freedom to sin has brought upon us. Like Dostoyevski's Grand Inquisitor in *The Brothers Karamazov*, we prefer happiness to freedom. We wish God had given us less freedom and had guaranteed that we would stay in Eden forever. We wish that He had put up a sign saying "No snakes in the grass", that He had given no law that we could ever have chosen to disobey. But that would not be father-love or mother-love, only smother-love. That would not be parenting, but patronizing and pandering. We would not mature but remain infants. What parent wants his or her child to stay an infant forever, even a happy infant? Mere kindness or compassion would keep us protected against suffering by denying us real freedom. That is the love we have for pets but not for persons, at least not persons we really respect. We are not meant to be God's pets. He did not create us for that. We are to be God's lovers. Our destiny is to be God's bride, and God is not a male chauvinist who patronizes us.

C. Redemption manifests love. The third part of God's love story, redemption, begins as soon as Adam falls. Genesis 3:15, the first Messianic prophecy, promises that God's love will never give up but will destroy the enemy's power through the "seed of the woman". Christ, Mary's son and Eve's offspring, is the New Adam, the Redeemer come to save us.

The Chapters in the Story of Redemption

Chapter One
Eden: Schooling

The great story of our redemption unfolds in stages. Some call these dispensations. In each, God initiates a covenant or two-party voluntary personal relationship, like a marriage contract. Each covenant has both a "letter" and a "spirit".

There is a clear verbal or written exterior to it and a supraverbal interior that touches on the things of the heart. The "letter" is a law, a verbal expression of God's will. It is a map for us to follow and obey. The "spirit" is always a matter of love. The reason for the letter—the reason for the law—is love. God wants to get us to marry Him. The law is a lovemaking manual.

The law in Eden is threefold. First, mankind is to "be fruitful and multiply". Second, the man and woman are to care for the garden. And third, they are not to eat the forbidden fruit, "the knowledge of good and evil". Each command comes from love.

Multiplying is love in two ways. First, in the obvious sexual way. Second, it is God's way of making many more of us to populate the earth. Now why would He want to do that? For the same reason He made any of us, of course. He loves us. Reproduction is the divine *Encore!*

Caring for the garden, the world He has given us, is training in love. God cares for the earth, and we are to learn to be like God. We are to learn how to love the world He has made. The world in this sense means a *place*, not a *time* or an era. It usually means the latter in Scripture. Thus "love not the world" does not mean we are not to love the *planet*—this beautiful material creation which God loved into existence. Rather, we are not to love this fallen, evil *age*, the spirit of the times. The word for "world" in the New Testament is usually *aion*: eon or era. The word for the "earth" is *ge*: the planet or the ground. It is important to remember the difference so we can respond to God's command to take care of the *earth* even as we oppose the *world*.

The point of the command to tend the garden (earth) is that God wants us to learn to love Him through loving other people and to learn to love other people through loving subhuman things. It starts at the lowest level with vegetables and fruits, then animals, then men, and then God. Love is not jealous. God wants to share as much of Himself and his love with us as possible, including His love for the earth.

And the forbidden fruit? That too was to teach us one of the precious lessons of love. I say "us" because the story of Adam and Eve is our story, too. We may wonder at the arbitrariness of the command, but that is the point, I think. Love is not content to obey only when there is some reason other than pure, blind, and loving trust in the beloved. If God had said, "Do not eat from that tree because it is poison", we would have obeyed for a double reason: trusting love and selfish fear. But God said, "Do not eat from that tree just because I say so." God gave us a command with no reason attached to it at all. Our faith and trust, love's two eyes, should have reached out gleefully at the opportunity for pure love, the opportunity to obey for only one reason. Here was the chance to obey not for any reason we see but only for the love we choose. What joy could have been found in this love lesson! But we flunked our first grade exam, and we've been in remedial summer school ever since.

Chapter Two
After Eden: Remedial schooling

A second covenant or dispensation comes after Eden. The exile from Eden—complete with the cherubim barring the way with flaming sword—is a severe mercy. But it is a mercy. For if we had been allowed to eat from the second tree, the tree of eternal life, in our fallen condition—if God had not imposed on us the loving penalty of death after we sinned—then all hope would have been gone. Then Hell incarnate would have reigned on earth. For that is exactly what Hell is: endless life without God, without love, with no possibility of return to the lost paradisaical relationship we abandoned in Eden, where God walked with us in the garden in the cool of the evening.

Thus all the curses pronounced after the fall are a blessing in disguise. They direct us back to God. Like the curses in Hosea 2 (read it!), they are God's whisperings of love to us in our wilderness exile, enticing us back to Him, our first and true love, by the hard way of suffering and death and the failure of our million little idols. If the prodigal son had not been starving in the pigsty, he would not have repented and returned to his father. The thorns and thistles that spring up after the fall prevent us from contentedly sleeping in our exile and mistaking it for home. They goad us back to God.

You see, God just will not let us flunk out of His school of love. He insists on remedial lessons until we get it right. For this whole world is a school set up by Love Himself to teach us to love. And Love Himself is absolutely imperious, demanding, and uncompromising. He simply never ever gives up. No matter what it costs us and no matter what it costs Him, Love will conquer all. Love will have its way.

Chapter Three
Noah: Radical surgery

When things went from bad to worse in Noah's time, God purified the human race. He saved us all by saving Noah and his family, the last good people on earth, and by destroying all the others. It is shockingly radical surgery, but it must have been necessary. For God does not perform needless surgery. In a world ruled by omnipotent love, every pain is necessary somehow, though the patient does not usually see how. How could he? The patient is not the doctor, and the sickness of sin has blinded the patient's vision.

The medical metaphor is apt because mankind is a body and not a machine. Each of us is a cell. The good and the evil of each affects the whole. Through the whole, each of us affects the good and the evil of every other cell in the body. That is why removal of the hopelessly diseased cells is necessary. We need to save the healthy cells before they become infected too. When only eight healthy cells are left in the body of mankind, it is time for radical surgery.

God sets up a new covenant after the flood. He promises that never again would such radical surgery be necessary, and He seals His promise with a rainbow. The flood, then, apparently a manifestation of divine wrath, was ultimately a manifestation of divine love. It is like the love of the cancer surgeon for the desperate patient, ruthlessly cutting out the cancer to save the patient. Now the prognosis is relatively good for the patient's future well-being.

Chapter Four
Abraham, the Father of the Faithful

The most important Old Testament covenant is with Abraham. "All the nations of the earth shall bless themselves by him" (Gen 18:18). The love God shows to Abraham and to his descendants, the Jews, is a problem to Americans because it seems so discriminatory. God chooses Abraham out of all others. The Jews are "God's chosen people". Is this love or arbitrary favoritism?

It is love, but it is also arbitrary favoritism! For love is arbitrary in the sense that it does not follow universal reason and justice. Instead, it is its own reason: "I love you because I love you." As Moses tells the people of Israel:

> "For you are a people holy to the LORD your God; the LORD your God has chosen you to be a people for his own possession, out of all the peoples that are on the face of the earth. It was not because you were more in number than any other people that the LORD set his love upon you and chose you, for you were the fewest of all peoples; but it is because the LORD loves you" (Deut 7:6–8).

And it is also favoritism, for love always plays favorites in the sense that the beloved is loved as someone special. God does not love you or me as a specimen of the human race but with the ravishingly personal attention and affection of a lover:

> As a lily among brambles,
> so is my love among maidens.
>
> There are sixty queens and eighty concubines,
> and maidens without number.
> My dove, my perfect one, is only one,
> the darling of her mother,
> flawless to her that bore her.
>
> (Song 2:2; 6:8–9)

To God *each* one of us is His favorite. God's love comes to all, but it comes to all as each, not to all as some anonymous aggregate.

Abraham is a paradigm for this kind of love. In choosing Abraham, God shows us how He chooses you and me. All who respond to His love call are His chosen people. The covenant with Abraham is the covenant with us if we are the spiritual children of Abraham, for then we share in his faith and hope and love. This covenant is promise, not law (see

Rom 4). In fact, it is the whispers of lovers planning their elopement. That is why Abraham obeyed when God told him to leave his hometown and everything he knew and loved. Only one thing can turn us away from what we love: a greater love.

Chapter Five
Moses: The Law

The law is an essential ingredient in the covenant. But until the time of Moses, God's law was only given interiorly. It was written on the heart or the conscience. With Moses, it is written externally for all to see on two stone tablets in the form of the Ten Commandments. Thus with Moses the covenant takes a new form. But it is still the same covenant relationship. It is like a marriage that exists before it is documented in the legal files at city hall. Moses is the archivist.

Law expresses and serves love. We do not usually understand that. That is why we do not understand the frequent exclamations of love and joy in the Psalms when the psalmist contemplates God's law: "His delight is in the law of the Lord, / and on his law he meditates day and night" (Ps 1:2). And again:

> The ordinances of the Lord are true, / and righteous altogether. / More to be desired are they than gold, / even much fine gold; / sweeter also than honey / and drippings of the honeycomb (Ps 19:9–10).

We do not understand this because we think of the law as a dead and as a threatening thing. But the psalmist thinks of the law as a living and loving thing. He recognizes it as the expression of the will of the living God, and His will to us is love. The law is the game lovers play. It is a serious and necessary game, but it is a love game. Take away the surrounding context of love—of two lovers' wills—and the law then becomes dead, impersonal, and threatening to your freedom. But lovers do not seek freedom. They seek to be bound forever to each other. Love naturally makes vows. Thus not only is love the fulfillment of the law (Rom 13:10), but law is also the fulfillment of love. That is why the Mosaic covenant of the law is also part of the love story.

The Mosaic law is like a nut with four layers of shell.

The outermost layer is the civil law: how to behave politically and publicly. This is determined by two things: (1) by the changeless principles of justice and the moral law (which is two layers down), and (2) by the changing situations and needs of a people in the process of moving through time, space, and history. Some of the principles of the civil law, like making restitution in kind for stolen or destroyed property, follow so directly from the moral law that they are binding for all times and places and societies. Others, like the Year of Jubilee when debts are released, are not. Some, like the law against usury (interest), are controversial borderline cases. Orthodox Jews, Muslims, and some Christians (Distributists, for example) believe this law is part of the natural law for all societies. Most Christians now disagree.

The next layer is the ceremonial law. It regulates public worship in the temple. What this temple worship with its elaborate animal sacrifices signified, as every Christian knows, is Christ. He is the real Savior, the High Priest, and the Mediator between God and man. That is why the mode of signification—the concrete symbols—were binding only until Christ came. The temple is gone. Animal sacrifices are no longer offered. Even Orthodox Jews cannot carry out all the letter of the ceremonial law.

The next deeper layer is the moral law, the Ten Commandments. These are rooted in human nature itself. Therefore they are unchanging and universal, for all societies and individuals. And, in fact, whatever lies your sociology teacher may have told you to the contrary, every society in history has had a moral law quite similar to the Ten Commandments. No society admires stealing or murder or adultery or lying or disrespect to parents.

The deepest law, the nut inside all three layers of shell, is what might be called the law of the heart. It is aptly expressed in the primary Jewish prayer, the *Sh'ma*:

> "Hear, O Israel: the LORD our God is one LORD; and you shall love the LORD your God with all your heart, and with all your soul, and with all your might" (Deut 6:4–5).

And: "You shall love your neighbor as yourself" (Lev 19:18). "On these two commandments depend all the law and the prophets" (Mt 22:40).

The point of the whole law is love. Love is the kernel of the nut. It is protected by the three layers of shell. Love is the law in a nutshell.

Love is the point of the moral law because each of the Commandments is a way of loving, a description of how love behaves. "Thou shalt not kill" means "Love does not kill." "Honor thy father and mother" means "Love honors one's father and mother." "Remember the sabbath day" means "Love remembers a sabbath day. Love takes time. It takes a honeymoon with the beloved." "Thou shalt not commit adultery" means "Love does not adulterate itself." The first commandment is the heart of them all: "Thou shalt have [love] no other gods before me" means "Love gives the whole of itself and tolerates nothing else before the beloved."

The ceremonial law, too, expresses love because it regulates acceptable worship. It assures a communion of love among members of the body with the beloved. Liturgical ceremony is a deed and a work. It is a yoke that binds the worker, like an ox, to his work of worship. And proper worship is simply the God-directed adoration of absolute love.

Finally, even the point of the civil law is love, for it heals the wounds that come from betrayals of love in a fallen society. Throughout the history of Israel, especially in the agonizingly detailed laws God gave His people, the divine Lover bends carefully over the wounds of His beloved and gradually performs His healing operation.

Chapter Six
The prophets

"And through the prophets taught [man] to hope for salvation", says Eucharistic Prayer IV of the Roman Catholic rite of the Mass. The prophets were and are God's mouthpieces—that is what the Hebrew word means—to remind His people of the love covenant.

The prophets are not progressives advocating a new order. Like the Church—which formulates creeds only to distinguish old orthodoxy from new heresies—the prophets hold God's Word against the stream of the spirit of the times, against the world, the reigning era, the new human fashion. The prophets call God's people back to their first love. Hosea 2 and Revelation 2:1–7 are good examples of this point. Notice that the prophets point backward, not forward, to bring back the wandering sheep to the loving arms of the shepherd and the security of the sheepfold.

The prophets also point forward to the Messiah. But in so doing they remind God's people of the Messianic promises already given of the future "day of the Lord" when the greatest act of love the world has ever seen would take place.

The prophets are like fingers, not like faces. We are not meant to look at them but to the reality to which they point. They all say essentially the same thing. It is the message relayed by John the Baptist, the last and greatest of all the prophets (Mt 11:11): "He must increase, but I must decrease" (Jn 3:30). Look at Him, not at me, they tell us as they point out the way.

The thing the prophets' fingers all point to—whether kindly or rudely, whether in the majestic, winsome poetry of Isaiah or in the rough, cranky doomsday talk of Amos—is the same awesome deed of love. They relate to us the unthinkable fact that God should so love the world that He would give His only begotten Son. In the prophets, as in the law, it is all love.

Old Testament history is full of threats, curses, violence, and war. The modern reader is likely to balk at the suggestion that this story is a love story. Isn't the Old Testament God the God of wrath and the New Testament Jesus the first to show God as a God of love?

No. That is a very old heresy. It is part of the Gnostic heresy of two gods. The Gnostics taught that the Old Testament Jewish God of wrath was opposed to the New Testament God of love who did not create the material world but redeemed souls from its awful clutches. This New Testament God of love was also thought to emancipate initiates from all law into a purely interior libertinism. He could only be known by a hidden and mystical knowledge *(gnosis)*. Sound familiar? Old heresies never die. They do not even fade away. They just change colors. They do not die, they dye.

The truth is that all the righteous anger and hard discipline of God in the Old Testament is just as surely love as is a mother's firm hand with a disobedient child in danger. It is not love to refuse to shout, "Get out of the street! There's a car coming!" It is not love to refuse to punish firmly and memorably the child who goes right ahead and does not listen but stays in the street. That would not be love but indifference, which is even farther removed from love than hate is because indifference does not even care.

But the Old Testament speaks of God's wrath as well as God's love. So does the New. What is the wrath of God then? Is it real or not?

It is real, but it is not part of God Himself. God is not half love and half wrath, or 99 percent love and 1 percent wrath. God *is* love. Wrath is how His love appears to us when we sin or rebel or run away from Him. The very light that is meant to help us appears to us as our enemy when we seek the darkness. The mother's embrace can appear as the worst imaginable torture to the angry child who wants only to fight. Thus some of the saints say the very fires of Hell are made of the love of God but experienced as wrath by the spiritually insane.

The Old and New Testaments reveal the same God. When Christ comes, He expects to be recognized by the people to whom God gave the Old Testament Scriptures. He expects the people who supposedly know the Father to recognize the Son: "Like father, like son." "You know neither me nor my Father; if you knew me, you would know my Father also" (Jn 8:19). And again: "No one who denies the Son has the Father" (1 Jn 2:23). Although the event of the Incarnation is a shock—indeed, the most shocking event that ever happened—yet the *character* of God revealed in Jesus is not meant to be a shock but a recognition and a fulfillment. This tough love is infinitely tender yet infinitely demanding. It is easy to please but hard to satisfy. That same consistent love is shown by God in the Old Testament and in the New.

Chapter Seven
Love's gospel

Each event in the life of Christ—each incident in the Gospels—is a note in the main theme of the love song. It would be possible to show this love at work in every detail and every event in the pages of the four Gospels. That would call for a much longer book, however. Instead, let us consider only the one supreme event of love. I am referring to the event to which each of the Gospels gives the most space and attention, the thing Jesus came for, the point of the whole story: I mean the Cross.

It is why He came, for He came not first of all to live but to die, not first of all to be a prophet or a teacher, or even an example, but to be the sacrificial Lamb of God, the Savior of a fallen world. He *is* the supreme prophet and teacher and example—the only perfect one in history. But even while He was living and doing these things, He was impatient to die. For that is what He came for, to "get the job done". It may seem strange to say that anyone was impatient to die. It may seem strange to say that Christ was impatient. But that is what He Himself said:

> "I came to cast fire upon the earth; and would that it were already kindled! I have a baptism to be baptized with; and how I am constrained until it is accomplished!" (Lk 12:49–50).

Here Christ speaks of "casting fire upon the earth" and being "baptized" two or three years after He was baptized by John the Baptist in the waters of the Jordan. Jesus is referring to the Cross.

What made Him so impatient? What fired Him so? Two things did. First, His love and obedience to His Father, whose will had sent Him on this mission; second, His love for us in our need. *Agape*, as we have already seen, is moved not by deservedness but by need.

Two of the things we needed absolutely were salvation from sin and knowledge of God and His love. Both of these were accomplished by the Cross.

Theologians have offered different explanations of *why* it was necessary for Christ to die, but what is certain in Scripture is that He did have to die if we were to be saved. Theologians have offered different explanations of *how* His death saves us. But what is certain in Scripture is that His death does save us: "With his stripes we are healed" (Is 53:5).

The Cross gives us not only salvation but also knowledge of salvation, not only God's love but also knowledge of God's love. If He had not done this unthinkable deed of love—a thing no saint, no prophet, no apostle understood or expected—how would we have known what perfect love is? What other event in history, what other concept that has ever been conceived, has ever told us what love is as radically as the Cross? The Cross is how Christ made the Father known most completely. The meaning of the Cross is the most complete exposition of John 1:18: "No one has ever seen God; the only Son, who is in the bosom of the Father, he has made him known." And: "In this the love of God was made manifest among us, that God sent his only Son into the world, so that we might live through him" (1 Jn 4:9).

Suppose you had an ant farm, and the ants rebelled against you. Suppose that somehow or other, the only way you could save the ants from the terrible results of their own folly was to become an ant and be killed by the rebel ants. How much love would you have to have to do this? Not nearly as much as God had. The distance He came, from the infinite to the finite, is infinitely farther than the distance you would have to go to become an ant. This remote and somewhat ridiculous analogy barely gives us a glimpse of the total shock and the utter surprise first felt by the disciples when they realized what God had done for them. Paul reflects something of this astonishment in Romans 5:7–8:

> Why, one will hardly die for a righteous man—though perhaps for a good man one will dare even to die. But God shows his love for us in that while we were yet sinners Christ died for us.

We could never have known how unthinkably large and wide and deep God's love is but for the Cross. Only through the Cross could it be "that you, being rooted and grounded in love, may have power to comprehend with all the saints what is the breadth and length and height and depth, and to know the love of Christ which surpasses knowledge, that you may be filled with all the fullness of God" (Eph 3:17–19).

The crucifixion was as much a sacrifice of love for the Father as for the Son. What loving earthly father would not far rather die himself than allow his beloved son to die? Although the Father does not become incarnate and suffer in time, although the Father's love does not take the form of sacrificial suffering as the Son's love does—that idea is the old "patripassian" heresy—yet the Cross reveals the love of the Father just as much as the love of the Son. After all, it was the Father who instigated the idea in the first place. The Son only obeyed the Father. He said, "I can do nothing on my own authority; as I hear, I judge; and my judgment is just, because I seek not my own will but the will of him who sent me" (Jn 5:30). The supreme proof of the supreme fact that God is love is the supreme event in all of history, the Cross.

Chapter Eight
The age of the Spirit

We are now in the age of the Church or the age of the Holy Spirit. Christ is still with us but not in the same form. His human body is in Heaven, but His Spirit still groans over the face of the waters of our darkness and sin here on earth. The coming of the Holy Spirit is also love. In fact, it is a deepening of love, for it draws God into even greater intimacy with us. Love seeks above all intimacy, oneness, insideness with the beloved. The human body of Jesus is external to us. It is separated from us by time and space, whether we were His contemporaries on earth or whether we have been born centuries later. But his Spirit is not external but internal.

The Incarnation was already a stupendous feat of intimacy. God did not just love us as an other but became one of us. Yet even this was not enough for Him, not enough intimacy. Jesus told His disciples that it would be better for them if He went away so that He could send His Spirit (Jn 16:7). Why is that better? Wouldn't we all prefer to have Jesus still with us physically? Wouldn't He draw a crowd of millions if it could be advertised that Jesus would appear in the flesh?

It might draw millions to stadiums, but it would not draw them far enough inside. He himself says it is better to have the Spirit. Why? Look at the difference the Spirit makes. Before the Spirit came at Pentecost, the disciples were still huddled in fear behind locked doors in the upper room. After the Spirit came, they went out to preach with incredible boldness and fearlessness and joy. They literally turned the world upside down. They had experienced the life-changing power of the Spirit.

Look at it this way. The Father is God outside you. The Son is God beside you. The Spirit is God inside you. Once God is inside you, you are spiritual dynamite.

What is that dynamite? What turned the world upside down at Pentecost? What made saints saints? What makes the cynical, skeptical world turn its head at a Mother Teresa? What made the hard-nosed Roman Empire convert to the religion of a crucified Jewish carpenter? The world did not say: "See how they explain one another!" but "See how they love one another!" The most effective argument for Christianity is Christians who are saints, lovers. The saints are the Spirit's salesmen. You cannot argue with a saint. He would just kiss you, as Jesus did to Judas and as He did to the Grand Inquisitor in Dostoyevski's parable in *The Brothers Karamazov*. How do you fight love? You don't. You lose. That is, you win.

Conclusion: The end of the story. The last stage in the story is the end of the story, the end of the world. As symbolically described in the last book of the Bible, Revelation, it seems to revert to Old Testament imagery of violence, judgment, doom, curses, fear, warfare, punishment, and wrath. But as we have already seen, even God's wrath is really only the face of love refused. If God's love is accepted rather than refused, then all the noise of battle becomes a love song, the triumph and glory and consummation of love. The military imagery is love imagery.

For the last event in history, according to the Bible, is a wedding feast. It is the supper of the Lamb, the celebration of the wedding between the Lamb and his Bride, the Church. That is, you and me. The point of all human history—the consummation of the plan that began with the Big Bang in Genesis 1:1 and steered us down a million mysterious side roads—is a marriage.

Just as in logic you understand why an arguer selects certain premises as evidence only in light of the conclusion he aims to prove, so in a story you understand all the events of the story only in light of the ending. You understand why the author selected these events and told this particular story only by knowing the point of the story, which is fully revealed only at the end. Otherwise, there is no reason to go on to the end.

And the story to end all stories—the story of human history and human life—ends for us (if we will it) with our marriage to God. Everything else—all the doom and gloom, all the sufferings and sadness, all the militarism and martial noise in Revelation, is like courtship, attraction, and foreplay. To some the image will sound irreverent, but it is chosen by the saints and by God Himself in Scripture. All our lives, God is waiting to make love to our souls. At the end, He does.

The Moral of the Story

That is, *if we will*. God is a gentleman. He cannot deny Himself. Love does not force itself on us. Love does not rape. Therefore, God will never force us, only entice us into union with Him. That is why Hell exists. The choice is ours.

The one and only absolutely important choice every human being who has ever lived must make is the choice between saying Yes or No to God's love, however dimly perceived. We are not saved by our clarity of head but by our charity of heart. Sometimes the choice will be so obscure, so invisible to human observers, that no one but God will have a clue as to the person's eternal destiny. Even in the apparently clear cases, the final secret is known to God alone. And our Lord informs us that some of the apparently first candidates for Heaven will be last, and the last first (Mt 19:30).

But however obscure it may appear to us, it is in itself absolutely black or white, Heaven or Hell, God or no God. There are no other alternatives. Infinite Love says, "Will you marry me?" And you either say Yes, or you don't. If you do, you are impregnated with the life of God. No one is ever half pregnant. Even if everything else in life seems gray, here is the one absolute black or white, either/or: the Last Judgment.

And what decides it is your love. "In the twilight of our lives, we will be judged on how we have loved", says John of the Cross, one of the great Christian mystics and lovers. From the beginning to the end, love is the guiding thread that leads us through all the labyrinths of time and life and history.

At the end, when we look into the eyes of our divine Lover, we shall see ourselves in totality, we shall see ourselves as He saw us and designed us from the beginning. At the end we shall touch the beginning. We shall hear Him sing to us something like the popular songwriter Dan Fogleberg's lovely song "Longer":

> Longer than there've been fishes in the ocean,
> Higher than any tree ever grew,
> Longer than there've been stars up in the heavens,
> I've been in love with you.

Jesus says something very much like this: "Then the King will say to those at his right hand, 'Come, O blessed of my Father, inherit the kingdom prepared for you from the foundation of the world'" (Mt 25:34).

The alternative is as unimaginably awful as this is unimaginably wonderful. The same one who says to the sheep on His right hand, "I knew you from before the foundation of the world" also says to the goats on His left hand, who have refused His love, "I never knew you; depart from me" (Mt 7:23). What unthinkable horror! God looks at you and says, "I never knew you."

How had they refused Him? "Truly, I say to you, as you did it to one of the least of these my brethren, you did it to me" (Mt 25:40). By the Incarnation, Christ has made Himself brother to all human beings. Henceforth, loving human beings is loving Christ. Thus the roads to the heavenly or hellish end of the story open up a thousand times every day for each of us: in the kitchen, in the office, in the car:

> And though there seemed to be, and indeed were, a thousand roads by which a man could walk through the world, there was not a single one which did not lead sooner or later either to the Beatific or the Miserific Vision.[3]

[3] C. S. Lewis, *Perelandra* (New York: Macmillan Publishing, 1944), p. 111.

7

God's Love in Systematic Theology: How God's Love Solves Theological Problems

Theology is traditionally divided into (1) systematic theology, (2) moral theology, and (3) ascetical theology or spirituality. For we can think about God (1) in Himself, (2) in our relationships with others, and (3) in our relationship with Him.

In each of these three divisions the love of God is so central that it solves otherwise insolvable problems. In fact, it solves the most burning problems. In the next three chapters we will sample how this is so. First, we will look at twelve problems in systematic theology.

1. Soft Love or Hard Dogma?

The very word "dogmatic" sounds about as acceptable to modern ears as "fascist". It connotes to that mind intolerance and persecution: the Inquisition. "Love", on the other hand, is the supremely acceptable word. To the modern mind it connotes something soft, something without hard corners or an unyielding nature and laws of its own.

Yet the love of God is a dogma.

A dogma, in Christian theology, is simply a datum. That is why theology can be a science. It has data. Data means "things given". A dogma is given or revealed by God, something we could never have discovered on our own. The older Greek word for it was *mysterion*, "mystery".

The love of God is a mystery because as Kierkegaard says, "If . . .God gave no sign, how could it ever have occurred to him [man] that the blessed God should [seem to] need him?" God must give a sign in order for us to know the surprising fact that God is not satisfied simply to be God, He has to be *our* God, too. Instead of being content to sit in the heavens and contemplate His own divine self-sufficiency, like the rational god of Greek philosophy, He bothers. He bustles around in history. He barges into our lives. The thought that God actively loves man may seem obvious to Christians, but that obviousness is an illusion of perspective. The idea is far from obvious in itself. It is a mystery, not a self-evident truth. It is a truth but not a truism.

The only reason we have for believing it is divine revelation—the very same authority that teaches other less popular and less comfortable dogmas like an objective moral law and sin and justice and Hell. Even if you discount the rest of the Magisterium—Scripture and Tradition—and accept only Jesus as your religious authority, the same conclusion follows: if you believe in the love of God because of Jesus, then you must also believe these other things for the same reason. If you deny them, then you should deny the love of God as well, because the authority of Jesus, Scripture, and Tradition is your only foundation for it. It is certainly not obvious to unaided human reason.

The conventional opposition in our experience and our thinking is between "soft" love and "hard" dogma. The dogma of God's love cuts through this conventional opposition like a sword through paper. In it the "soft" (love) becomes as hard as eternity, and the "hard" (the eternal God) becomes as soft as a mother cuddling her baby.

2. *Justice versus Mercy*

An opposition similar to the "soft-versus-hard" one is "justice-versus-mercy". In human affairs, justice and mercy are seen as an either/or. If the penalty owed by law is exacted, justice is done and not mercy. If it is not exacted, mercy is done instead of justice. But God's love is both just and merciful. There is no break between the two.

Because justice and mercy are two unchangeable attributes of divine love, both have to be satisfied, or rather expressed. (We must not speak as if God had a problem satisfying two conflicting demands that came to Him from some quasi-external source.) If God had destroyed mankind after the fall, that would have been consistent with His justice but not with the whole of His nature, which includes mercy. If He had simply said, "Forget it, it doesn't matter. I won't exact punishment", that would not have been consistent with His nature either, because justice has as eternal a stake in God's nature as mercy and vice versa.

Since God's dealings with us necessarily reflect His nature, they must reflect both justice and mercy without compromising either. The crucifixion of Christ was His way of manifesting both completely. The Psalm (85:10–11) prophetically foretells this when it says:

> Mercy and truth are met together;
>   righteousness and peace have kissed each other.
> Truth shall spring out of the earth;
>   and righteousness shall look down from heaven (KJV).

In the first two lines, mercy and justice (truth) are reconciled. In the last two, Heaven and earth are reconciled, tied by this double rope.

We moderns often tend to forget eternal necessities since our lives are surrounded by human artifices, changing and changeable things. We forget that justice is an unchangeable necessity and not a man-made law. God's love has a structure. It is righteous and just. It is *right*. It is not sentimentality. Because the modern mind does not see this, it does not understand why God could not have simply said to us, "Forget it." After all, wasn't it cruel and unnecessary for God to require the death of His Son?

No. For justice, or moral necessity, is as necessary as mathematical necessity. It simply could not ever be right to treat sin in the same way as holiness, any more than it would be right to treat a minus number as a plus number. God could not do that simply because God is truth and not deception.

The modern mind also forgets that God's mercy is not like man's mercy. It is not optional and changeable, but as necessary and eternal and unchangeable as His justice. We tend to have an image of two gods, or at least of two contrary halves of God. We think of his justice as part of His unchangeable divine nature but His mercy as part of His changeable human nature, something He assumed with the Incarnation.

No. It is the eternal Father who out of His mercy sent His Son. The Son reveals not only Himself but the Father: "He who has seen me has seen the Father" (Jn 14:9). God's mercy has as great a claim staked in the ground of His eternal essence as does His justice. Indeed, if any distinction can be made, mercy is *more* primordial than justice (see Thomas Aquinas, *Summa Theologica* I, 21, 4). Insofar as the distinction is valid at all, justice is how His mercy appears rather than vice versa. But, ultimately the distinction is valid only on the human mind's side of the prism where the white light of God's absolute oneness seems to diverge into different colors. It is ultimately false because in God justice and mercy *are one thing*, rather than two things reconciled. They are simply two aspects of God's love.

3. How to Know God

How is it possible for man to know God? For finitude to know infinity? For imperfection to know perfection? For fallen, sinful, selfish, and fatally flawed souls to know the all-holy and all-heavenly One "who sits enthroned above the cherubim" (1 Chron 13:6), who "dwells in unapproachable light"?

Jesus' answer is this: "Blessed are the pure in heart, for they shall see God" (Mt 5:8). A pure heart means a single heart, a heart in which only one desire lives: love.

Love knows God. But the knowledge of God that we can have in this life through love is imperfect for two reasons. First, our love is flawed. Second, it is finite.

Sin flaws love and therefore flaws knowledge. Even if our *agape* comes from God, it is poured into broken vessels. Our love is the mirror in which God appears, but our mirrors are cracked and dirty.

But even if we had not fallen, even apart from sin and its consequences, a second reason for the imperfection of our knowledge of God is that we are finite. Only a finite image of the infinite God can appear in a finite mirror. The only mirror that reflects all of God is God. The only one who knows the Father perfectly is the Son.

This, too, is due to love. It is because only the Son loves the Father infinitely that He knows Him perfectly. The unfallen angels know and love God better than the best saint, but still their knowledge is finite.

Let's look at this second reason, our finitude, more closely to see how the traditional answer to the question of knowing

God becomes intelligible only through love. The question is: how is it possible to know God at all if He is so transcendent as to be not on our level of being at all? He is being itself, self-sufficient being, while our being is essentially dependent and derived. So how can our minds latch on to Him?

The traditional answer is by analogy. When we say "God is good", we mean something analogous to human goodness. We do not mean something wholly the same nor something wholly different. If the meanings were wholly the same, God would be reduced to our level; if they were wholly different, there would be no connection at all and thus no knowledge. If we claimed to know God as we know human things, we would be pagans; if we said we did not know Him at all, we would be agnostics.

The traditional answer certainly seems necessary and right. But it must be added that the primary analogy we have—the most adequate analogical ladder by which to climb from human experience to some likeness of God—is that of love. The love in our lives is not only the most important thing *morally* but also the most important thing *intellectually*.

Since love is God's essence, we know God better by knowing love than by knowing anything else. Just as the sun's nature can be known better from the sunbeam, which *is* sunlight, than from the tree or the coal, which is *caused* by sunlight, so God can be known best from the *agape* in our lives. It is the same sort of stuff, though the difference between infinite divine *agape* and finite human *agape* is far greater than the difference between the finite sun and the finite sunbeam. But it is a valid analogy. Our thought and our hope and our love can travel up the sunbeam and aspire to the sun. We can fly with the wings of aspiration and hope along the sunbeam of *agape* to the Son of God.

4. Does God Change?

If we assume that love is a process, a change, then we must choose between believing (1) that God is unchanging and therefore not really loving; or (2) that God is love and therefore in process and in time, not eternity. Is God in time or not?

God is eternal. Scripture suggests, Christian tradition generally teaches, and reason confirms that a God in process would be an inferior God. A God who is still growing better or worse—or at least a God who does not possess all of His being at once—is clearly imperfect. A God whose life is partly in the dead past or in the unborn future is not total life. Whatever "eternal" may mean, it means not-that, not-temporality. God's eternity has to be affirmed.

But how can a timeless God love? The only meaning we can assign to love is that of a temporal process, is it not?

No. The essence of love is not a process but a spiritual act. "Act" does not necessarily mean "temporal activity". It can mean an eternal, timeless act. Indeed, a timeless act is *more active* than a temporal act because a temporal act has *potentiality* (maybe-ness, could-be-ness) mixed in with it. It is not wholly actual. The present alone is wholly actual. The future is only potential. The past is no longer either actual or potential, but dead. It lives only in present memory. If God were in time, He would have a future, which is only potential, and a past, which is not even that. In that case God would not be wholly actual. Even we could imagine a more perfect God than that.

But we cannot imagine a more perfect God than God. Therefore God must be wholly actual. That means He must be eternal. But God is love. Therefore love is in essence wholly actual and eternal.

Love is the most active, actual reality. It *becomes* a temporal process when it enters the medium of time, but in itself it is simply an act.

This is extremely difficult to conceive and impossible to imagine because all our experience is temporal and our imagination is limited by our experience. It is possible, however, if we are careful, for our conception to go beyond our imagination, then we can avoid the error into which we would otherwise fall. Because we habitually think in terms of the time we experience, we easily make the mistake of supposing that the only two alternatives for God are a process of active change in time or a state of changeless inactivity in time. But neither applies since God is not in time. A static state is just as much in time as a process. In it, nothing changes *while time goes on*, as a rock stands still in a rushing river. Yet time does not flow past God. He does not exist in time; therefore, He must not be imagined to exist in a static state.

God is first. He originates, invents, and *creates time itself.* In Scripture, God is never passive. He speaks. He questions. He challenges. He plans. He initiates. He acts. He is always the one who loves me before I ever knew of Him or loved Him. I am essentially the responder; He is essentially the initiator.

Agape, unlike the other three natural loves, is like God in that way. *Agape* is not a receptive, responding process but an initiating, creating source.

The practical importance of this abstract doctrine of love's eternity is this: if we did not know that God is love, we would think God is eternal by being static rather than dynamic and active. Then we would not know that God is love. Or else we would think God is dynamic by being temporal rather than eternal. Then we would be stuck with an imperfect God. *Agape* overcomes the dilemma.

The doctrine of the eternity of God's love also solves another very difficult question. If the blessed in Heaven know that there are damned souls in Hell, how can they be happy? Logic analyzes the problem as follows: they either know it or not. If not, then they are ignorant, which is not heavenly. If so, then they either love the damned or not. If they do not, they are loveless, which is not heavenly. If they do, then they are sad, which is also not heavenly. Therefore, there is either ignorance or lovelessness or sadness in the blessed in Heaven. In any case, Heaven is not heavenly.

The answer to this trilemma is that the blessed share in the same kind of knowledge and love for the damned that God has. They share His purely active *agape* rather than a passive feeling. Feelings are always hostage to events for their joy. When her little baby girl holds her breath, mommy sweats and frets. When a teenage boy cracks up the car, dad's "How could you do this to yourself?" always means also "How could you do this to me?" With us, *agape* is always mixed with the other loves. Unselfish love is always mixed with our needs. But God has no needs, so His love can be wholly unselfish. It is purely active, not passive to events, not dependent on events, not hostage to events. Its joy cannot turn sour or sad. And this joy will be given to us: "He will wipe away every tear from their eyes" (Rev 21:4).

So do God and the blessed love the damned? Yes. But this love does not demand to be reciprocated at the price of its own happiness, any more than the light demands to be reflected by a mirror at the price of its own illumination. Light is still light whether it is reflected by a polished mirror or absorbed into an opaque object. God's joy is like that. It does not depend on us, nor does His knowledge of our lapses diminish it. And our joy will not be diminished by what we know about the damned. How could Hell eternally blackmail Heaven?

The reason we cannot successfully imagine this heavenly state of consciousness is that in our present experience *agape* needs feelings of sympathy and compassion as its consort. It would be not only impossible, but also inhuman for us to love without feeling, without passivity, without being able to be hostage to others' blackmailing our joy. Look at the Man of Sorrows! He made Himself perfectly hostage, wholly blackmailed when He was on earth. But there are no sorrows in Heaven.

Though we cannot *imagine* a state of pure eternal gift-love, we can surely *think it*. We can distinguish in our thought the two different ingredients in our present mixed loves: the active, giving element and the passive, needing element. And our reason instructed by faith can run ahead of our imagination when we think of God and the blessed in Heaven. If it does not, we are like pagans and our Heaven is only Valhalla or the Happy Hunting Grounds. We should certainly be able to believe what we cannot imagine; "Eye hath not seen, nor ear heard, neither have entered into the heart of man, the things which God hath prepared for them that love him" (1 Cor 2:9, KJV). But, the text goes on to say, God has revealed precisely these things to us.

6. Why Pray if We Cannot Change God?

Another practical question that can be answered by our distinction between divine, eternal *agape* and human, temporal loves is the question: Why pray for anything if God is eternal and already knows everything we need and everything we will get?

God knows as present what to us is future. So God knows at the moment I pray exactly what will happen and whether I will receive the thing I pray for or not. I cannot change God's mind since God is not passive, He is not pushed around by me or anything else. But since I cannot change God's mind by praying, why pray?

This problem applies only to petitionary prayer, of course. A high-minded answer might be to say that petitionary prayer is the lowest form of prayer and ought to be replaced as we mature by a pure, disinterested adoration and thanksgiving instead. But that would be contrary to the teaching and practice of Scripture and of Christ. We are commanded to ask God to help us and others who are in need. Why?

Pascal answers: "God instituted prayer to communicate to his creatures the dignity of causality" (*Pensées*). God lets us really cause events and really make a difference not only by physical work but also by spiritual work. If you say that we should not pray because God already knows our needs, then you must say that we should not farm or eat or read for the same reason. We should no more stop the one than the other on the grounds that God knows the future. *We* do not know the future. God does not need our prayers or our works, but *we* need both.

Further, what God knows *is* precisely our activity, both of work and of prayer, physical work and spiritual work. To stop it because God knows it already is to say God can know it without it being there for God to know, which is self-contradictory.

But we still cannot change God, can we? No, we cannot. But is *that* why we pray? To change omniscient Love? Isn't it rather to learn what it is and to fulfill it? Not to change it by our acts, but to change our acts by it.

The fact that God's love is unchangeable does not change the fact that it is *love*. It always wills what is best for us. And prayer is best for us. Therefore, we must pray precisely *because* God's love is unchangeable. He is unchangeably loving and commands prayer for us.

Prayer is no illusion. God's will and ours really do touch and interact in prayer, not in the way that a human father's and son's do, but in the way that the divine Father's and Son's do. The ultimate dignity of prayer lies in the astonishing fact that through prayer we share in the very life of the eternal Trinity. When we pray to the Father, it is through the Son and moved by the Spirit. When we pray to the Son, it is the Spirit of the Father that moves us. When we pray to the Spirit, it is the very love between Father and Son that is both the subject and the object of the prayer. Ultimately, prayer is Trinitarian love.

7. Freedom and Predestination

If God is not love but only knowledge, then it is difficult or impossible to see how human free will and divine predestination can both be true. But if God is love, there is a way.

Freedom and predestination is one of the most frequently asked questions among my students—partly because of modern man's great concern for freedom, but also, I think, for the largely unconscious reason that we intuitively know both these things must be true because they are the warp and woof of every good story. If a story has no plot, no destiny—if its events are haphazard and arbitrary—it is not a great story. Every good story has a sense of destiny, of fittingness, as if it were written by God. But every story also leaves its characters free. Lesser writers may jimmy and force their characters into molds, but the greater the writer the more clearly the reader sees that his characters are real people and not just mental concepts. The more nearly the characters have a life of their own and seem to leap off the page into real life, the greater a writer we have. God, of course, is the greatest Writer of all. Since human life is His story, it must have *both* destiny and freedom.

Let's look first at the side called destiny. Predestination is a misleading word, I think, for it concedes too much to our temporal way of thinking. God is not *pre or post* anything. He is present to everything. God does not look down rows of dominoes or into crystal balls. He does not have to wait for anything. Nor does He wonder what will happen. Nothing is uncertain to Him, as the future is uncertain to us. There is not *pre*destination but destination, not *predestiny* but *destiny*. This follows from divine omniscience and eternity.

But our free will follows from the divine love. To love someone is to make him free. To enslave him is always a defect of love.

Now since divine love is God's very essence, while omniscience and omnipotence are only attributes of that essence, therefore *if* one of these two truths had to come first—in the sense of being more primordial and non-negotiable than the other—it would have to be freedom.

I do not think either truth needs to be compromised. I think we can do as much justice to the sovereignty of God as a Calvinist and as much justice to the free will of man as a Baptist. Yet it would not compromise the very *essence* of God to deny predestination. Arminianism, the theological view that denies predestination and emphasizes the role of man's free will in receiving grace from God, may be wrong. But it is wrong at a relatively technical, theoretical level. Denying human free will, on the other hand, would cut out something immediately essential to the Christian life: personal responsibility. If I am a robot, even a divinely programmed robot, my life no longer has the drama of real choice and turns into a formula, the unrolling of a prewritten script. God loves me too much to allow that. He would sooner compromise His power than my freedom.

Actually, He does neither. It is precisely His power that gives me my freedom. Aquinas reconciles freedom with predestination by saying that God's love is so powerful that He not only gets what He wants, but He also gets it in the way that He wants. Not only is everything done that God wills to be done, but it is also done in the way He wants it to be done. It happens without freedom in the case of natural things like falling rain and freely in the case of human choices. A power a little less than total may get what it wants without getting it in the way that it wants it. But omnipotence gets both. And the way omnipotence wants human acts done is freely.

In other words, freedom and predestination are two sides of one coin. The omnipotent Author chose to write a story about free human beings, not just trees or machines. That means we are really free. We are free precisely *because* God is all-powerful.

If love and power were not one, we would have the classic standoff, an unending conflict between the two. Once you see the center, love, everything else falls into place like spokes in a wheel.

The oneness of love and power is also why we need not fear God's power: it *is* His very love. Therefore, it *cannot* be used lovelessly. And it is also why we need not fear that His love will ever fail, for it is omnipotent. It *is* power. The very hands that tossed the galaxies around like grains of sand loved mankind so much that they let mere men nail them to the Cross, all for love. The One who loved us even unto death, the supreme weakness, is infinite strength.

In fact, if we only believe and remember the unity of these two things, God's love and God's power, if we only believe in the two attributes that can least be subtracted from God, the practical result will be the most revolutionary transformation of joy and confidence imaginable, life-changing. To see this, all we need do is reread Romans 8:31–39. "What then shall we say to this?" What is the inevitable consequence of the fact that the omnipotent God loves us so much that He "did not spare his own Son but gave him up for us all"? Simply this: "Will he not also give us all things with him?" It follows as the night the day that not "anything else in all creation, will be able to separate us from the love of God". No, it follows even *more* surely than the night follows the day, for the laws of physics will change before the laws of God's nature ever will.

If God is all-powerful and all-loving, then "in everything God works for good with those who love him." Even in persecution, torture, and death! For although "for thy sake we are being killed all the day long", yet "in all these things we are more than conquerors." Why? Because these tortures, like everything, serve the one single end of the single-minded and single-hearted God who wills only our good. He practices what He preaches: purity and simplicity of heart, 100 percent love. The only way out of His love is not chance or suffering or death, but deadly sin. And even past sins can work for our good through present repentance. If only we will it, everything works for our good because everything is God's love. It is so simple that only a child could understand it, or one who has become like a child. "I thank thee, Father, Lord of heaven and earth," said Jesus, "that thou hast hidden these things from the wise and understanding and revealed them to babes" (Mt 11:25).

8. Love and Christian Unity

It almost goes without saying that if we realize God's love and live it, we will heal the divisions and brokenness within

Christendom. *Only* if we realize God's love is this possible, for no merely theological reconciliation is enough. The tragedy of denominationalism arose through a lack of love, not only a lack of knowledge or theological orthodoxy. Indeed, we cannot even understand what orthodoxy is without love, for orthodoxy means right belief about God. And God is love.

We split God's visible Church (no one can split the invisible Church) because we were selfish. We decided to be our own conductors rather than all following the divine baton. That has to be the root cause of denominationalism, for God is peace and unity, so if we all loved and obeyed and followed His leading, we would necessarily sing in harmony. We are not singing in harmony, therefore we must have disobeyed Him, disobeyed love. The diagnosis is inescapable.

And so is the prescription. Though a thousand further details need to be addressed, here is the most important ingredient of all in the prescription for reunion. Here is the root of all true ecumenism. All churches and denominations must approach dialogue with purity and simplicity of heart. They must seek not triumph or power or self-justification or conversions but simply to follow God's will. If that were done, a miracle would happen. Impossible healings of our divisions would become possible. Reunion without compromise would happen. And the world would once again sit up and say, astonished, "See how they love one another!"

9. "Comparative Religions"

One of the most important areas of theology in our time is comparative religions, for the most common of all objections against the Christian religion is that it is *a* religion. People say it is only one of many and has no right to make exclusive and imperialistic claims to truth. We moderns tend to feel that it is narrow-minded to claim that one religion must be wrong and another right even if the two contradict each other. In that case, Jesus must have been narrow-minded when He said, "I am the way, and the truth, and the life; no one comes to the Father, but by me" (Jn 14:6).

In most other religions, especially Oriental religions, God is impersonal. At most, God is consciousness but not will. That is why these religions have no absolute moral law. Judaism alone among the religions of the ancient world identified the object of worship with the origin of moral law. Christianity and Islam inherited this concept of God from the Jews, their fathers and teachers in faith. In all three theistic Western religions, God is will and person. His name is I AM. In Eastern religions, the *I* (self, ego) is the supreme illusion that must be dispelled through mystical enlightenment. In the West, the human *I* (self) is the image of God, the most real one of all. How could two ideas be further away from each other?

Ego, will, love, morality, law, obedience, sin, justice, punishment, individuality, freedom, responsibility, and Hell are all part of the package of doctrines that make up biblical theism. Every one of them is denied or transcended in classic Vedanta Hinduism and Theraveda Buddhism. They are seen through as illusions or used temporarily as myths for inferior levels of consciousness.

Because there is no God spoken of at all in Buddhism and only a god that is an impersonal cosmic consciousness rather than an individual loving will in classical Hinduism, therefore, in these religions human love is seen only as a means for purifying consciousness from selfishness and preparing one to climb the mystical ladder of enlightenment. At the top of the ladder, love disappears. The following statement is not extreme or atypical: "The true Buddhist does not hate, and in the end he cannot hate. For the same reason, the true Buddhist does not love and in the end cannot do so."[1]

Now how could students of comparative religions possibly miss this crucial difference? How can they claim that at their core all religions are the same, unless what they are really saying is that, as G. K. Chesterton put it, "Christianity and Buddhism are really very much alike, especially Buddhism"?

What Buddha means by love is only attachment or selfish love. He calls this *tanha*. He does not either affirm or deny *agape*. He simply does not know it. In other words, he does not know God. He may know the depths of the human soul, and we may want to turn to him for some deep psychological insights, but not for theology.

If God is love, not all religions are the same because not all religions know that primary fact.

10. Hell

Can we relate even Hell to God's love? It is the most unpopular of Christian dogmas and the one most widely disbelieved, even though Jesus clearly taught it on many different occasions. It is disbelieved mainly because it seems to most people to contradict the dogma of God's love. And *if* we have to deny one of the two, then of course let's deny Hell. Hell without God's love is ... well, just Hell. God's love without Hell is still God's love.

But in fact the two do *not* contradict each other. Far from contradicting God's love, Hell manifests God's love. It is the other side of the coin of God's love.

[1] Eugen Herrigel, *The Method of Zen* (New York: Pantheon Books, 1960).

To make this clear, we must first distance ourselves from false and unnecessary popular pictures of Hell as a frying pan or a torture chamber, especially from the picture of a wrathful God deliberately throwing reluctant human beings into Hell against their will just because they were bad, or because they were not good enough for Heaven. This picture is false in at least four ways.

First, God does not throw people into Hell. We throw ourselves in. Divine judgment simply reveals what is already there. We make Hell for ourselves when we refuse Heaven and God and joy. Whether or not there is an external place called Hell (why not?), it certainly begins and ends in our own hearts.

Second, the notion of going to Hell against your will denies free choice. But the only reason Hell exists at all is because of free choice. And that in turn exists only because of God's love. Thus God's love is the ultimate reason for Hell's existence. The premise of God's love results in the conclusion of Hell through the medium of free choice. If you love someone, you give him his freedom. God could have created good little robots, and then there would have been no Hell because there would have been no real persons. Because God loved free persons into existence, Hell became possible.

Third, I strongly suspect that what goes to Hell is not the kind of thing we would recognize as a human being at all if we saw it. It is more like ashes. A damned soul is one who has made an ash of himself. Hell is fire. Fire burns and destroys. Just as what goes to Heaven is more human than it ever was on earth, what goes to Hell is less human than it ever was on earth. It has lost its soul, its center, its self, its I, its humanity, its personality. It has become "legion" (Mk 5:9). Compared with a person, it is what a thousand slivers of broken glass are to a mirror. It deserves not hope or prayers or pity, for there is nothing there any more to pity or to love, only dust to sweep into the dustbin. If time still held us in its grip in Heaven, we would remember what this thing once was—a person—and regret that it had not fulfilled its potential. But in Heaven all is actual and present for Heaven is our participation in God's life, and in God all is actual and present. There is no regret or fear over what might have been or still might be.

Fourth, you do not go to Hell for being bad. This comes as a tremendous shock to those who have never read the Bible or who have read it through the eyes of sleep or prejudice. It is incredible to see how many people have read the Bible and heard sermons all their lives and still missed the most important point of all, how to get to Heaven! They persist in the natural illusion that we can earn Heaven by brownie points, that God is the tabulator of our debits and credits, a divine accountant rather than the divine Savior. If that were so, either all would go to Hell or the cutoff point between the Heaven-bound and the Hell-bound would be arbitrary. Would 999 good deeds or 100 bad deeds merit Hell, but 1,000 good or 99 bad deeds merit Heaven? That is not even justice, much less love.

So how *do* you get to Heaven? If I do not buy that answer, what is my answer?

Wrong question. My answer is no better than yours. How about both of us listening to Jesus' answer?

It consists of two words: "repentance" and "faith". "Repentance" means turning away from sin, anti-God attitudes and acts. "Faith" means believing and receiving God's gift of His Son Jesus, the Savior of sinners. The only thing that can keep us out of Heaven is not sin but refusal to accept God's cure.

You see, since God's love is infinitely actual and not passive and potential—not dependent on things outside it—it is not dependent on our worth. It is not a response to our worth. It creates our worth. As Saint Thérèse loved to say, "Everything is a grace."[2] God does it all, in Christ; we only have to accept it.

Of course, once we do, God's life in us will make us act differently. Faith saves us, but good works follow. The same Bible that says we are justified by faith also says that a faith without good works is dead, fake faith.

But God loves us not because of our good works. God *just loves us.*

That does not mean there is no Hell, since love means freedom, and freedom means the power to say Yes or No, and that means the power to say No even to God.

11. Love and Particularity

One of the most popular heresies in the Middle Ages, imported from Greek and Islamic philosophy, was that God knows and loves only universal species and concepts, not individual persons. It stemmed from Aristotle, who thought God would demean Himself by caring about mere individuals, so He occupied Himself with nothing but contemplating His own perfection. That was the only object worthy of His attention. In other words, Aristotle's God had his nose in the air. But the God of the Bible has His nose to the ground. He works. He cares. He gets His hands dirty. He broods over His people like a mother hen, like a Jewish mother—because He is love and love is always particular.

But particularity also sounds snobbish to many people. How dare the Jews claim to be the chosen people? The

[2] Thérèse of Lisieux, *Last Conversations* (Washington, D.C.: Institute of Carmelite Studies, 1977), p. 57.

Incarnation itself has been called by some universalist scholars "the scandal of particularity". How dare God be so discriminatory as to pick out individuals for special merit? Not the rest of the world, but Abraham; not Ishmael, but Isaac; not Esau, but Jacob. And Moses, Mary, Peter, and Paul. Throughout Bible history God is *not* egalitarian. This is particularly hard for Americans to accept.

According to a poll conducted by a Georgetown professor, most Catholic college students consider themselves Americans who happen to be Catholics rather than Catholics who happen to be Americans. But God is not an American!

The reason God is not an American is that God is a lover. Americanism—in the sense used here—is essentially the ideal of equality, and love knows nothing of equality. As we see in the Song of Songs, to the eyes of love the beloved is *not* equal to others but unique. If comparison is made at all, the beloved is always the best. But love does not compare, it just loves.

The lover does not love his beloved's eyes because they are perfect. They are perfect because he loves her. He does not love her because she has beautiful black hair. He loves black hair because: "Black, black, black is the color of my true love's hair."

But then what becomes of universality? That is also a divine truth. God loves not just some but all. But He loves all individually. Put abstractly, the problem is this: we want both concreteness and universality. We want neither a love that stops with the abstract universal nor a love that stops with only one concrete individual, but a love that is both concrete and universal.

Hegel's solution was to start with the universal, which is the philosopher's temptation, and to declare it concrete. His god knows and loves "the concrete universal". Like Plato,

Hegel thought that abstractions like humanity or the state were things in themselves. He thought they were more real than individual things and were the proper objects of belief and love for both God and man.

The Bible's solution is just the reverse. Scripture starts with the particular and then universalizes it. You are called to love your concrete individual neighbor and then to realize that every individual is your neighbor. The point is not to destroy concrete neighborhood in a fit of universalism but to expand the local neighborhood and embrace the universal neighborhood.

This is exactly what parents do with their children. They love them all, but they love them each. That is why *Father* is the best earthly analogy for God. If it isn't, why did Jesus use it? Good parents are not particular in an exclusive way by loving this child but not that one. Nor are they universal in an abstract way by loving all in general but no one in particular. Rather, they are universally particular by loving each totally and specially. Love works by a wholly different mathematics than the mathematics of finitude, in which equality becomes division. In math, if I give you half, I have only half left for myself or for another. But love gives all to each and loses nothing.

12. Practical Hermeneutics

How are we to interpret Scripture? Are there universal rules? Love again provides the way.

The first principle of interpretation, everyone would agree, is *contextualism*. A passage must be interpreted in context. If this is not done, nearly anything can be proved from any passage. But the context is not just the immediate context but also the entire context of Scripture. That is, the ongoing story and revelation of God, including the personality of the God who reveals Himself.

We know the meaning of the text by the context and the smaller context by the broader one. But when it comes to the broadest context—the meaning of the whole Bible and the nature of God—how are we to know the truth? There are so many different competing interpretations, especially of the big picture. A second principle that answers this question is the principle of *objectivity*. To understand the passage, understand the context, and to understand the context, especially the broader context, be objective, open, and honest. Do not interpret the book in light of your own ideas or your pet prejudices. Look at yourself in its light, not it in your own light. Look through the author's eyes and not your own. Do *not* interpret the book—any book—in light of your own sincerely and honestly held beliefs. Interpret the book in light of the *author's* beliefs. *That* is what sincerity and honesty means in hermeneutics, in the science of interpretation. To do the opposite confuses *interpretation* with *belief*, confuses the author's ideas with your own.

Any good author will write clearly enough so that if the reader does his part in being open and honest, the intention of the author will come through. It is rare, of course, to find a wholly honest reader. Our second principle is violated constantly. But it is not an impossible task, or even a terribly difficult one. It just requires an honest and sincere attempt of will, rather than special gifts or training of the intellect.

But the overall context of the Bible is the nature and designs of God, and God is a person. A person can be known only by personal understanding, not impersonal understanding. Personal understanding takes place through love, caring, willingness, intimacy, and relationship. So our third principle must be: in order to obey the second principle and to understand the

God who is the overall context of the Bible, you must be open to God. You must be personally engaged. You must be, in a sense, *subjective*. To be objective (principle two), you must be subjective (principle three). *Thus love is the basis for interpretation.* Just as Jesus says, "If any man's will is to do his [God's] will, he shall know whether the teaching is from God" (Jn 7:17). That is why saints understand the Bible best: they are great lovers.

8

God's Love in Moral Theology: How God's Love Solves Ethical Problems

God has no moral obligations. He is under no law. He is the source of law. Thus moral theology does not mean the study of God's morality but of man's morality in relation to God. In the study of man's morality, our love for God rather than God's love for us is the focus. This is because God's love for us does not follow a law, but our love for Him does. In fact, to love God is "the great and first commandment" (Mt 22:38). So in this chapter our main focus turns from God's love for us to our love for God.

1. What Does It Mean That "Love Is the Fulfilling of the Law"? (Rom 13:10)

The moral law is the expression of God's will. Our love for God is the expression of our will. Thus our obedience to God's law is the love affair in which our will meets His. Earthly obedience is thus an imperfect version of heavenly bliss. Our ultimate bliss in Heaven comes not, as the pantheist mystics think, from a confusion of substances but from a harmony of wills. That is the formula Saint Bernard of Clairvaux uses to define our final destination.

Harmony with God's will, obedience to God's will, does not mean merely avoiding sin, nor does it mean only doing all the things the law tells us to do. Obedience here means not just obeying the *law* but obeying the *will of God* behind the law. And since that will is love, obedience is our yea-saying to love.

Obedience without love is not what God wants. The deeds of love without love are not what God wants, as we saw in our reflections on 1 Corinthians 13. Feelings of love without love are not what God wants, for feelings are love's accompaniment and not its essence. Service to His Kingdom, even to the point of "delivering up my body to be burned" (martyrdom) without love is not what God wants. Moral purity, even sinlessness without love is not what God wants. Even salvation, attainment of heaven without love—if, contrary to fact, that were possible—is not what God wants. First Corinthians 13 could not possibly make the point more strongly. Without love nothing else has any value.

What, then, does God want? Simply, He wants what any lover wants. He does not want merely the fruits and effects of love but our love itself, our hearts. He wants *us*. The lover, in some mysterious way, wants the beloved herself. His object is not to possess her, not to have power over her, not even just to enjoy the pleasures she can give, but he wants her herself. Love longs for union, however dimly it is understood and however impossible it is to explain. Love longs for perfect harmony of wills but not confusion of substances. That means the union in which the two become one without ceasing to be two. This is the crazy, impossible, but true mathematics of love.

God wants our will, our heart, and our freedom. When He gets it, He gives it back multiplied. "He who loses his life for my sake will find it" (Mt 10:39). This is the ultimate law of morality because it is the ultimate law of reality, of the nature of God, the origin of all reality. It is the unchangeable pattern of the Trinity-in-love by whom everything is created.

Once we obey this law, once we give our heart to the Heart of reality, then the other segments of the circle of our lives will fall into line around the center. First comes the heart, the will (the free chooser). Then the mind, the understanding. Then desires, which must be instructed by the mind. Then our time, our very lives, our whole lifetime. (How hard it is for us in this hurried and busy age to give God *that*! But our time is precisely our lives.) Then our speech, our very words, for in our words we shape our worlds and give them meaning. Then our relationships, our horizontal loves. Finally, our death. If we consecrate these seven things to God, we fulfill His will and our purpose in living. And that is the point of morality.

2. *The Solution to Sin*

God's love for us is the solution to sin. God's deed of justification on Calvary and of sanctification at Pentecost—the Father's sending us His Son and His Spirit—this is the first and necessary cause of the conquest of sin. But our response in love to God is also part of the solution to sin since "love is the fulfillment of the law."

The link between God's step one (His love for us) and our step two (our love for Him and for neighbor) is our acceptance of God's love and our faith in it. This is the revolutionary movement of our souls from fear to faith. It is the definitive liberation from the curse of the law which Luther discovered so powerfully when he read Romans.

Faith is simply our acceptance of God's love in Christ. Faith is the alternative to sin: "Whatever does not proceed from faith is sin" (Rom 14:23). Faith must therefore be first of all an act of will rather than of intellect. Faith is fundamentally saying Yes to God. Sin is fundamentally saying No to God. That is why they are the exclusive alternatives.

According to Genesis, the origin of sin was first of all a lack of faith. The whole drama takes place in the will first of all. Adam and Eve chose to accept doubt rather than faith. That was the first step in the fall, as in every sin. We choose to believe the devil's lie rather than God's truth. The serpent first offered Eve the option to doubt God's word (Gen 3:1—"Did God say . . .?"). Then and only then followed the disobedient deed (3:6). The heart rebelled before the head and the head before the hand.

The first question is: Whom do we choose to believe? Whom do we trust? To whom do we entrust our heart? That is, whom do we love? Love determines faith. Faith is not an intellectual opinion arrived at by abstract reasoning. It is a lived relationship of trust with a person arrived at by love and will, choice and freedom. That is why we are personally responsible, even eternally responsible, for our faith or our faithlessness.

When we believe God is something other than a lover, it is inevitable that we will sin. The devil tempted Eve to believe that God was selfish, arbitrary, and jealous in forbidding the forbidden fruit. Perhaps God was even evil, the devil implied, for he described God as "knowing good and evil" (3:5). This "knowing" probably means *experiencing* good and evil—as Adam "knew" Eve in Genesis 4:1, for example. Once Eve began to believe that God might not be pure love, an opening for sin was created. If all of me believes that God loves me, then nothing in me would want to disobey Him. The way to conquer sin, therefore, is to build up faith in God's love.

3. Law, Love, and Union

One of the things we mean when we say that love is the fulfillment of the law is that when we do not love a person, it is difficult or impossible to fulfill the moral law with respect to that person; but when we love someone, it is possible, even easy, even inevitable, and positively delightful to do what the moral law commands us to do to him. It is hard to do good deeds for one you despise, but a joy to do the same deeds for one you love.

But our innate selfishness runs counter to love. We do not have *agape* or unselfish love by nature. *Agape* is supernatural. So we need some sort of real contact with God, who is the source of *agape*. We need some real union in order for this love to come into our lives. You can see God's strategy. First, He drives us deeper than law into love, for only love empowers us to obey the law. Then, He drives us even deeper, toward contact and union with Himself, for only He can transform our selfish natures into love natures like His own. Like a sheep dog driving the sheep ever closer to home, He drives us from law to love and from love to union.

This union with God can come about only by a "new birth", a death of the "old man" and a birth of the "new man" (Jn 3:3; Eph 4:22–23; Col 3:9–10). The two selves—selfish and unselfish, unloving and loving—are opposites like fire and water. When one is born, the other must die.

The new birth, in turn, comes only by faith, just as pregnancy comes only by a woman's body receiving a man's seed. Faith is our reception of God into our soul. The new birth is our spiritual pregnancy.

Thus moral theology leads us four steps deeper than law. To fulfill the moral law, we need love. To get love, we need union with God. To get union with God, we need the new birth. And to get the new birth, we need faith.

4. The Trinity of God-love, Neighbor-love, and Self-love

It is well known that the twofold law of love to God and neighbor includes all other laws. But it is not as well known that these two laws, which include all others, also include each other. But this is necessarily true, for you cannot love your neighbor without getting love *(agape)* from God, and you cannot love God without obeying His command to love your neighbor.

There are two common errors about the relationship between these two fundamental moral laws. Both errors attempt the impossible task of separating the two. But like an organism in symbiosis, each half dies without the other. Loving God without loving neighbor—whether this is self-absorbed, private mysticism or self-justifying, Pharisaical legalism and ritualism—always ends up in loving a false god, perhaps even a demon. And the same is true of the opposite. The attempt to love man without loving God also turns sour, even demonic, as we have seen with the many atheistic totalitarian regimes of our modern times. These regimes always claim the mantle of the love of man—whether Aryan man, proletarian man, Turkish man, or ideologically pure Marxist man. In each case, Jews, bourgeoisie, Armenians, Chinese revisionists, or Cambodians are brutally slaughtered by the millions. The hypocrisy is always quickly unmasked. The slaughter of some is *not* done for the love of others but for the love of raw power.

Only secularists should be surprised at that. The fact is that only God-lovers are real man-lovers. Only saints are saintly. There is no answer to the agonized question of the

French existentialist and novelist Albert Camus' alter ego Dr. Rieux in *The Plague:* "How is it possible to be a saint without God?" No argument will convince one who does not believe this, but experience will, whether firsthand or vicarious. Read the memoirs of those who have experienced the godless love of man firsthand. Read Arthur Koestler's *Darkness at Noon*, or Czeslaw Milosz's *The Captive Mind*, or Armando Valladares' *Against All Odds*.

Not only must you love God to love man, but you must also love man to love God. Those who burned men for love of God did *not* burn men for love of God, but for fear, hate, or power. For "as you did it to one of the least of these my brethren, you did it to me" (Mt 25:40).

Dostoyevski captures that truth stunningly in his parable of the Grand Inquisitor in *The Brothers Karamazov*. The inquisitor is willing and eager to burn Christ Himself when He returns to earth amid the Spanish Inquisition, for the sake of the inquisitor's version of the love of mankind. For Christ upsets and challenges mankind, offering the terrifying freedom of choice between good and evil. By contrast, the inquisitor offers security, contentment, and relief from the burden of responsibility and freedom. Since the inquisitor identifies love with kindness, he is perfectly logical in claiming to love man more than Christ does. Thus the burning of men for the love of God (the Inquisition) becomes the burning of God (Christ) for the love of men. And that is exactly what happened the first time on Calvary. The inquisitor's philosophy is only that of Caiaphas the high priest: "It is expedient for you that one man should die for the people, and that the whole nation should not perish" (Jn 11:50).

There is great depth and mystery here to unravel and explore. But one thing is clear and simple. The two things must go together or not go at all. Loving man and hating

God means hating man. Loving God and hating man means hating God. Atheist inquisitors and religious inquisitors make the same mistake.

Loving others is also inseparable from loving *self*. If you do not love yourself, you cannot love your neighbor *as* yourself. And if you do not love your neighbor, you do not really love yourself, for the self's good and growth comes only through loving neighbor. When we sacrifice self for neighbor, *we* grow. When we exalt self over neighbor, *we* shrink.

Every family and every nation knows that from experience. The message of the prophets and moralists is no head-in-the-clouds idealism but is shown true every day. Sacrifice for the poor, and you prosper. Get greedy, and you lose all. The way to your own success and happiness is to forget all about success and happiness and to practice love and justice to others instead. The reason for this paradox is that self, others, and God are connected in an inseparable love trinity.

The connection between love of God and love of neighbor is more internal and necessary than simply obedience. It is certainly true that if you love God you will want to obey Him. And since He commands you to love your neighbor, out of that love of God you will love your neighbor. But the connection is more intimate than that. It is this: to love God is to *enter into* God and to let God enter into you. It means actually to share God's life and let Him share yours. But to let God enter into me is to let God's love for my neighbor enter into me.

In other words, loving neighbor means not only coming under God's law but coming into God's life. It also means coming under God's law but in a deeper sense than obeying the precepts. Law in Scripture sometimes means not just precept or prescription, but also a principle or origin of living. The Greek word Paul uses in Romans 8:2–6 is *nomos*. "The law of the flesh" is death; "the law of the Spirit" is life. There is the same real, objective, and unbreakable connection between love of God and love of neighbor as between sin and death. Death is not an arbitrarily chosen punishment for sin. Death is the necessary consequence and outworking of sin. Death *is* sin that has run its course. So love of neighbor *is* love of God that has run its course. The very same life of divine *agape* comes in us at one end, so to speak, as love of God and out the other as love of neighbor. Only our illusion of perspective makes us see *agape* as if it were two things.

5. Honesty

Why should I tell the truth?

We are to tell the truth rather than to bear false witness to our neighbor. Speech is a social act. Speech is a relationship. If I love my neighbor, I will his good. And truth is the good of the mind as food is the good of the body. I want truth for myself. Many want to deceive, but no one wants to be deceived. If I love my neighbor as I love myself, I will want truth for him too. Therefore I will be honest with him.

There are two motives for lying, and only love casts both out. The first is selfishness, the desire to benefit at my neighbor's expense. I desire to do unto others what I would not want them to do unto me. The second is fear. I fear being misunderstood, rejected, put down, or hated. Love casts out both selfishness and fear (1 Jn 4:18). Therefore love casts out lies.

The devil is "the father of lies" (Jn 8:44), and in casting out his children we cast out the father. Love is exorcism. The devil absolutely cannot endure two things: truth and love. They are the two things God Himself is by His essence.

And these two are one. Love is not a correction to truth. It is not as if truth were hard and hurting but love soft and easy. Love does not falsify the truth for the sake of easing the hurt. The first act of charity we can do for our neighbor, says Aquinas, is to tell him the truth. But it must be "speaking the truth in love" (Eph 4:15). This "in love" is not a modification of "the truth" but of the "speaking" of it. In fact, it is not even a modification of speaking in the sense of a loving falsehood; love is the very life of truth. Paul's point is *not* that we should hold some truth back out of love. Rather, it is to speak the truth *because* that is the loving thing to do.

Of course the truth is not simply identical with the facts. Facts are only one kind of truth. It may be a fact that your neighbor is fat and ugly, but it is not telling him the whole truth to simply tell him that fact boldly. It is also not your business unless you are his confidant, parent, doctor, dietician, or beautician. It is also true that he is loved by God and therefore lovable to God. That means he is lovable to you and should be loved by you. Tell him *that* truth, in many different ways. That truth does not contradict but transforms the fact that he is fat and ugly.

6. Power

"God is not in strength but in truth", said Gandhi. When relations of power become uppermost in our calculations in affairs of state, family, or Church, then the state, the family, or the Church begin to disintegrate. Even affairs of state should be love affairs. In the long run, the supposed weakness of love is the only lasting power (cf. 1 Cor 13:8–13).

That is still true. Hitler's power did not last, but Gandhi's did. Where is Caesar's power today? And where is Christ's? Machiavelli said, "Armed prophets succeed; unarmed prophets fail." But Machiavelli himself succeeded only as an unarmed prophet, a writer.

Where is supreme power? In God. What is God? God is love. There is no escape from the conclusion that, ultimately, love is the only real power.

7. *Peace*

More than ever before in history we need peace in these times of nuclear weapons and terrorist ambitions. One way that claims to be a way to peace is pacifism. Pacifism has been one tradition in Christendom among others, but it has never become official teaching, except among small groups like the Quakers. The Catholic Church calls it "an honorable option" for some but not a moral requirement for all.

I do not believe in pacifism as an ideology. I think pacifism idolizes peace. If you absolutize peace you will not find peace. But if you make peace relative to God and His will—whose will may lead to conflict, even armed conflict if necessary to deter a bully and defend peaceable victims against aggressors—then you will find God's peace, the only lasting kind. According to the beatitude, peacemakers are children of God (Mt 5:9). All in the family—like father, like son.

If you seek God's peace, "the peace the world cannot give", (Jn 14:27) you will find it, according to His own promise. "Seek and you will find" (Mt *7:7)* applies only to God and the divine attributes, one of which is "the peace the world cannot give". But if you seek only worldly peace, you will not find it: "I have not come to bring peace, but a sword" (Mt 10:34). And: "I have said this to you, that in me you may have peace. In the world you have tribulation; but be of good cheer, I have overcome the world" (Jn 16:33). Seek the world's peace at any price and you will not find it. You will find only Chamberlain at Munich and then Hitler at Warsaw.

This is a hard saying to modern absolutizers of political solutions: trusters in horses and chariots (Ps 20:7) and bombs, *and* to trusters in treaties banning bombs. But Scripture is embarrassingly clear: to get peace you must go to where it is, its source. And that is not the fallen human heart but the Heart of God, which is perfect love.

8. *Peacewaging*

The world is divided between the wagers of war and the admirers of peace. We must develop a third attitude: the waging of peace.

The wagers of war have the wrong *ideal*—war. But they have the right passion and the right excitement in the waging. On the other hand, the admirers of peace have the right ideal of peace. But they lack the passion, the energy, and the excitement of the war-wagers. We need to enlist the warlike mentality of passion in the service of the ideal of peace. Peacemaking, peacewaging must become our war.

Life *is* warfare: spiritual warfare. "For we are not contending against flesh and blood, but against the principalities, against the powers, against the world rulers of this present darkness, against the spiritual hosts of wickedness in the heavenly places" (Eph 6:12). An essential weapon in this warfare, Paul says in one of the next verses, is "the gospel of peace" (v. 15). Peace and war are not wholly separated. All the excitement of military strategy, all the commitment of a campaign, all the life-or-death urgency of a battle, can and should attend our consciousness of peacewaging.

And when do we fight this great battle? Every day. Every moment. Right now. In every ordinary day-to-day decision to resist temptations to anger, lust, laziness, revenge, cowardice, and selfishness. We must open our eyes to what is going on, to the war in our own backyards and kitchens and living rooms. It happens wherever and whenever two persons interact in any way. There is the battlefield between light and darkness, sanctity and sin, self-giving and selfishness, love and lovelessness, God and Satan, Heaven and Hell.

9. Family

What can be said about this crucial area of the battlefield that has not already been said? Wise observers know our civilization is dying because its basic building block is dying. That building block, the family, is dying because the love that is its glue and foundation is dying. That love, in turn, is dying because it comes from God, and God is no longer at the center of the modern family, even most modern Christian families. There is a more drastic decline in the number of Christian families today than in the number of Christian individuals.

Secular man finds this diagnosis of our civilization's troubles an intolerable and incredible imposition of religious dogma upon experience. Such an objection is like calling the doctor's grave diagnosis that cancer is causing you to lose weight and will kill you unless you let him operate an intolerable imposition of an alien scientific ideology upon your body's experience.

Storge depends on *agape*. Familial affection will go sour if *agape* is not present. Just as the organs die when they no longer receive blood from the heart, families die when they no longer receive the blood of *agape* from the heart of God through the body of Christ. And when our families die, our society and civilization dies.

The prescription for healing is the reverse side of the diagnosis of the disease. Even Confucius knew that when he said in the *Analects:*

> If there is peace in the heart, there will be peace in the family. If there is peace in the family, there will be peace in the nation. If there is peace in the nation, there will be peace in the world.

He needed only to add: if there is peace with God, there is peace in the heart. The Trappist monk Thomas Merton, writing on the spiritual life, completed the diagnosis: "We are not at peace with others because we are not at peace with ourselves, and we are not at peace with ourselves because we are not at peace with God." That just about says it all in one sentence.

To save civilization we must save the family. To save the family, we must save *agape*. To save *agape*, we must go where it is and get it at its source.

10. *Work and Career*

Everyone makes three fateful choices in life: a God to worship (or not to worship), a mate to marry (or not to marry), and a career to work at. Something is very wrong with our civilization in the third category as well as the first two. Marx's critique of capitalism has power to it (though his cure is much worse than the disease) because he sees that most people in the modern West do not love their work. They are alienated from it. They no longer refer to it as a "calling", as they did in the past. Today it is only a "job". No longer is what you do seen as the important thing but only how much money you make. This is indeed alienation from work.

Love restores work. You do not have to *like* your work to love it, just as you do not have to like a person to love him. If you believe in your work, you can love it, for faith and love are twins. But if you do not believe in what you do, you cannot love it, for you really think it is just unnecessary busyness or the unnecessary making or advertising or marketing or distributing of silly luxuries. And then half your waking life becomes subtle economic slavery.

What is the connection between the love of God and the love of one's work? Simply that with the love of God comes the love of the human part of that work. If your work is in line with human nature as God designed it, then you can love it because you can love God in and through it. Its activity can image God's activity. Because that activity is love, your work can be love. You can love God in it, and God can love you in it.

But if you cannot bring your work to God and God into your work, this cannot happen. By bringing God into your work I don't mean sharing religious testimony during work, but doing your work well and with pride for God's sake. You sanctify carpentry not by praying before each cut of the saw but by cutting well for God's sake. No sloppily made benches ever came out of a certain carpenter's shop in Nazareth.

There are some jobs in our world that it is difficult to bring God into. That is the deepest problem of work in our world: the love of God is not in it.

11. *Education*

There is one simple key to exciting and successful education on any level. It is not methods, contents, curricula, plans, institutions, teacher training, integration with experience, job training, social relevance, or any of the other cures we have spent so much time and money trying. It is one thing: good teachers.

Good teachers, in turn, means two things, both of them love-things. The teacher by whom students are inspired, the teacher who changes their lives, is always a double lover. He is a lover of the subject and a lover of the student. Students detect that love almost infallibly, and it is simply irresistible.

Good teaching is not even a matter of super-special intelligence. Think back. Wasn't there some bright, clever teacher you were unmoved or turned off by and therefore never deeply educated by? Wasn't there some other teacher who was much less than a genius but who had caught the spark of the enterprise, the wonder of learning, and passed it on to you? The first teacher may have taught you a thousand things, but you forgot them because they were little things and they didn't come wrapped in love, the greatest preservative. The other teacher taught you a few big things, and you will never forget them. They came wrapped in love, winged with the passion that you learn this precious thing. You and your learning were precious because they were loved.

This is especially true about teaching values, the most important and controversial of all things taught. Socrates seemed to think in the *Meno* that values ("virtue") could *not* be taught. This is to say, in effect, that whatever is teachable is not worth teaching and whatever is worth teaching is not teachable. According to Socrates, you could not teach values, only remind the student of his innate knowledge of them so that he could teach himself.

It is a half truth, I think. Values cannot be taught as a code can be taught, but values can be caught as a cold can be caught. How do you think twelve ordinary fishermen learned the value of *agape* and became apostles and saints? They caught the Spirit from the Teacher. The Spirit is love. This is a paradigm situation, not an exception to be filed away as a dusty specialty labeled "religion". It is the key to all teaching. Teaching abstract values is not enough. The spirit of love must be passed on.

But this love of student and subject that is the key to great teaching is a love of God, at least implicitly, even if the teacher is an agnostic or an atheist. The spark is not just natural affection, friendship, or desire but some sort of disinterested, self-forgetful, wondering, and worshipful *agape* for the student and for the subject. For the student is an image of God, who is love, and the subject is a bit of truth, which God is also. Loving these two supreme values of personhood and truth is implicitly loving God because *that is where they are*. They are divine attributes. Therefore good teaching is loving God.

12. Money

Because money can buy everything money can buy, it represents the whole world beneath us, the world we can control. It represents the world of things that do not have free will, the world of non-persons. Why is it true that "the love of money is the root of all evils" (1 Tm 6:10)? And why did Jesus warn against greed more than against any other sin? Because the dictum "Love people, use things" is the fundamental moral wisdom; and "Love things, use people" is the fundamental moral stupidity. Greed is that stupidity.

Yet our whole economic system is based on greed. According to John Locke, whose ideas have influenced our system more than any other thinker's, private vice can produce public virtue. The profit motive—which used to be called "greed"—will make everyone work harder and produce more wealth, which will trickle down to all, so everyone will be wealthier and happier.

But it is one of the most well-known and well-ignored platitudes in the world that riches *do not* make you happy. In fact, rich people are by and large less happy than poor people. The suicide rate is almost *inversely* proportionate to poverty. There is more joy among the poor of Haiti or Calcutta than among the rich of Hollywood or Manhattan. If this seems outrageous to you, check it out. Visit. See for yourself. Or talk to those who have.

The key, again, is love. What do the poor have in Haiti that the rich don't have in Hollywood? Love—either love of God in himself or indirectly in his image, our neighbor. Even the image of God, like the shadow of Peter (Acts 5:15), is powerful enough to perform miracles, to make the desert valley of poverty wet with joy (Ps 84:6). Saints were many things, but two things none ever were: joyless and greedy. Many were sorrowful but none were joyless. And not all were poor in money, but all were poor in spirit. There are no yuppie saints.

13. Sex

Everyone knows we are a sex-obsessed society, but not everyone knows the reason. Put simply, sex is for most people a search for love, or even a substitute for love rather than an expression of love. Most of the moral issues people feel deeply about today concern sex: abortion, divorce, premarital sex, family disintegration, homosexuality, and feminism.

Addicts cannot see clearly. Addicts have little sales resistance. These two facts explain (1) why the media that depend on advertising also hate and fear traditional religion and (2) why greed and lust go together in our society.

Our society *needs* sexual obsession to sell its luxuries. Drop sex from advertising, advertising from capitalism, capitalism from economy, economy from politics, and politics from our society; and our society has nothing left. To obey either "Thou shalt not covet thy neighbor's wife" or "Thou shalt not covet thy neighbor's goods" would be the two most radical, destructive programs you could ever let loose in our society. Just as greed and lust are subversive to love, love is subversive to greed and lust.

Greed and lust are obsessions, but love frees. Love is not an obsession. You make sex free when you join it to love. Marriage does that. It sexualizes personal love and personalizes sexual love. Monogamous, lifelong marriage makes sex free.

Take heart, all you who prefer freedom to obsession. Our obsessive society will not last. Nature, like the body, rejects alien organisms. Only love lasts (1 Cor 13).

What we Christians are doing here is spy work, building a future supernatural Kingdom in the middle of the present temporary one. Our citizenship is elsewhere. We are "strangers and exiles" here (Heb 11:13). Not only when we live in specifically Christian ways but even when we practice the old pagan virtues like self-control in a society that laughs at such quaint antiquities, we are the true revolutionaries and futurists and progressives. The Kingdom we are building will last when this moribund one dies.

But if the body of sexual love is informed with this soul of *agape*, it too partakes of eternity. When sex is a dimension of love, it comes into the Kingdom. Perhaps one of the great developments of modern theology, and a witness to our age, which needs it so desperately, will be a glorious new theology of sex.[1]

[1] This sentence was originally written in 1988. Since then we have seen exactly what it hopes for in Pope John Paul II's "theology of the body".

9

God's Love in Practical Theology: How God's Love Solves Spiritual Problems

This division of theology is traditionally called "ascetical theology". But that term connotes hair shirts and long fasts to modern minds rather than simply "spiritual discipline". The currently popular term "spirituality" is also misleading, I think, because it sounds Gnostic, as if emancipation from matter rather than from sin were the point. So I have called it "practical theology." But let us not quibble about labels. Let us relate the love of God to twelve specific problems within this division of theology, which studies our inner life, our individual relationship with God. The last chapter explored *agape* in our horizontal relationships with others; this chapter will explore *agape* in our vertical relationship with God.

1. *Eros*

As used in Plato's dialogues and as it comes down through the ages into current usage, *eros* means something more specific and more passionate than simply "desire" in general, but also something less specific and less limited than simply the desire for sexual experience. "Passionate desire" is perhaps its best translation.

Following C. S. Lewis' usage in *The Four Loves*, let us use a separate word (he uses the word *Venus*) to refer to the merely biological sexual element in *eros*, the thing we share with the animals. *Eros* includes *Venus* but also includes more. The most common instance of *eros* is romantic love or falling in love—something that goes far beyond mere animal desire. Think of the magnificent obsession that is romantic love—all the passion of joy and selflessness it includes. Can *eros* teach us something about *agape* and the love of God?

Indeed it can. Remember how it felt being in love? Then remember that God is everything the beloved seems to be and infinitely more. We will feel no less in love with God in Heaven than we do with the beloved now. This is a sorely needed corrective to the conventional, cold, pale, and passionless pictures of Heaven that usually fill our brains and dull our desires.

The ancients called *eros* a god sent from Heaven. I think they were not totally wrong. I think *eros* can be a teacher, an intimation and foretaste of something of the Beatific Vision of the true God. I think that is one of the reasons why the marriage relationship is so sacred to Christianity. This is why when it goes bad it can do so much harm, in accordance with the principle: *Corruptio optimi pessima*, "The corruption of the best things is the worst."

The ultimate source of all love is heavenly. *Eros* is heavenly love received into a certain earthly medium. It is a prophet far from his home country, prophesying a consummation that is far off, a fulfillment that is not to be identified with the prophet himself. This is often done: we mistake the pointing finger for the fulfillment, *eros* for *agape*.

Eros brings great joy, perhaps more than any other earthly thing in our lives. The only greater joy is the joy that is one of the fruits of the Spirit. That is why the following remark of Aquinas about joy is one of those simple sayings that can simply stun you when you hear it. If you have experienced the passion of *eros*, it is one of those sayings that you will never forget because it suddenly illuminates and explains a whole dark, mysterious area of your life:

> No man can live without joy. That is why a man deprived of spiritual joy goes over to carnal pleasures (*Summa Theologica* II–II, 35, 4 and 2).

We are designed for joy. Joy is our fuel, our food. When true fuel, true food, is missing, it becomes psychologically inevitable that we go after false fuel, false food, which cannot satisfy.

Why is it that "no man can live without joy"? Because we are designed by Joy for joy, because "the serious business of heaven is joy."[1] What we were created to do and experience eternally in Heaven is the joy the saints anticipate here on earth.

The word "ecstasy" comes from the Greek *ek-stasis*, which means "standing outside yourself". The key to ecstatic joy is standing-outside-yourself, self-forgetfulness. All peak experiences have that feature. Once we turn around to look at ourselves, we spoil it. We want to lose ourselves in it, like swimming in an ocean. *Eros* is so powerful mainly because it is an image of that self-forgetfulness, that yielding bliss.

In self-forgetful joy we can accomplish things we could not accomplish before. This is true even physically. Saints, spies, and soldiers have gone without sleep or food for many days because they were passionately in love with some ideal, if only saving their lives. Every great act of intuitive discovery—every mental act that cannot be controlled by the conscious ego

[1] C. S. Lewis, *Letters to Malcolm: Chiefly on Prayer* (New York: Harcourt Brace Jovanovitch, 1964), p. 93.

but comes from the deeper, larger world of our unconscious—is an act of self-forgetfulness.

That is one reason why humility is the first virtue. Saint Augustine said that the four cardinal virtues were "Humility, humility, humility, and humility". That is because humility is self-forgetfulness. It is not self-hatred or putting a lower value on yourself than you deserve. It is not inaccurately low self-regard or even accurately low self-regard, but rather self-regardlessness, self-forgetfulness.

We need humility so badly that God often allows other sins to persist in our lives and to bother us badly when He sees that if He gave us the grace to overcome them, we would fall into the worse sin of pride and lose the joy of humility. Aquinas says that God thus acts like a doctor who tolerates a lesser illness in a patient when necessary to cure or prevent a greater one.

He does it for love, not just for humility. Humility is a means to love. Love cannot happen without humility and self-forgetfulness. One reason God allows sins that He could prevent is because the one who has been wounded by sin, even by his own sin, often loves more, forgives more, and is more humble. Mary Magdalen is an obvious example. Look how close she was to Christ after she repented. Christ said of her, "Her sins, which are many, are forgiven, for she loved much" (Lk 7:47).

That does not mean, of course, that her particular sin, which was prostitution, is easily forgivable because it was motivated by love. Prostitution is *not* love. Rather, it means that she was forgiven because of her great love of God's mercy, which led her to repentance. This also gave her a deep appreciation for forgiveness, a deep gratitude. For "he who is forgiven little, loves little" (Lk 7:47). The conclusion is certainly not that it is better to sin more so that we can appreciate forgiveness more—that is like saying we ought to hit ourselves on the head with a hammer because then we will appreciate more how good it feels when we stop—but that God allows us to sin in order to draw us from pride to humility, gratitude, and appreciation. Above all, God wants to lead us to love. Love is "the one thing needful" (Lk 10:42).

2. *How to Pray*

Prayer is not fundamentally a transformation of consciousness or meditation. It is not even fundamentally a lifting of the mind to God. That is only its necessary preliminary. Prayer is fundamentally a transformation of will, a lifting of the heart and will to God. Thus prayer is ultimately identical with sanctity, or the wellspring of sanctity. Prayer is ultimately a way of doing that for which we were made, namely, that death of self, that self-forgetfulness, which is the heart of *agape*. It is the ecstatic joy of dying to self and identifying with the beloved instead. This is done most centrally in the will. We should therefore pray more with the will. The best prayer is to say with our whole heart Mary's *Fiat* (Lk 1:38): "Let it be to me according to your word", Your *will*. This is the simplest and shortest prayer conceivable, the essence of prayer, the perfect prayer. One word: *Fiat*, our Yes. It is so simple that nothing more needs to be said.

3. *The Fear of God*

The thing that the Word of God calls "the beginning of wisdom" (Ps 111:10) is the thing that nine out of ten religious educators today agree is the one thing that most stands in the way of religious maturity, the one thing that most assiduously must be extirpated from the minds and hearts of the young: the fear of God.

Which authority shall we listen to? "Let God be true though every man be false" (Rom 3:4).

But we must understand this divine word. What *is* "the fear of the Lord" that is the beginning of wisdom, and how is it related to the love of the Lord that is the end of wisdom?

It is not servile fear, fear that my enemy will harm me or fear that my cruel master will take advantage of me. It is awe, worship, and adoration of God as my friend but not as my chum. It includes the understanding that God can be terrible even though He is good—"terrible" meaning not "bad" but "great and high and holy".

I think there is not a single experience in the storeroom of human consciousness that has more catastrophically disappeared in the modern world than this. I know no other way in which the modern Western mind more radically differs from the kind of mind that prevailed at virtually all other times and places in history than this: the loss of awe.

Most people confuse this holy fear with servile fear, or else they make the distinction by defining nonservile fear simply as *respect*. No, that is far too weak a word. It is holy terror. Words alone will not convey it. If any do, they will probably be something like those of Charles Williams in his novels that convey a real sense of the supernatural, or those of C. S. Lewis in *The Chronicles of Narnia* because of the feeling Aslan evokes. Aslan, the great lion in Lewis' fantasy, may well bring you closer to Christ than any other literary figure, for many feel about Aslan the awe they could not feel about Christ. Then they can transfer the feeling to its true rather than its fictional object. I know of no catechism text that can perform this most essential task of religious education for the young better than *The Chronicles of Narnia*. I know two teachers who have used it with startling success. I recommend it to anyone who teaches religion.

Even *servile* fear is necessary at the beginning of religious education. "Perfect love casts out [servile] fear" (1 Jn 4:18), but if there is no fear to cast out, love cannot do its work and attain its full flower. The love of God without the fear of God, as Kierkegaard says, is trivial:

> In order really to love God it is necessary to have feared God. The bourgeois' love of God begins when vegetable life is most active, when the hands are comfortably folded on the stomach, and the head sinks back into the cushions of the chair, while the eyes, drunk with sleep, gaze heavily for a moment towards the ceiling.[2]

The love of God without the fear of God is not true love but a sentimental convenience, an animal love. But the servile fear of God without the love of God is no better. It is also an animal thing. To rise above both animal fear and animal love, we must join fear and love in *agape*.

God's love has two faces, and our love for Him must reflect both. God's love is both kind and severe, both merciful and stern, both compassionate and authoritative, both forgiving and demanding, both soft and hard. Again, in George MacDonald's words, God is "easy to please but hard to satisfy".

Everyone knows the first of these two faces today, but few know the second. In the past, most knew the second and fewer knew the first. (I am not nostalgic about "the good old days.") Few know that the two are one, that the very absolute, unchangeable, eternally necessary attribute of God, the thing He cannot compromise, is precisely His

[2] Søren Kierkegaard, *Journals*, in *A Kierkegaard Anthology*, ed. Robert Bretall (New York: Modern Library, 1946), p. 11.

compassion and mercy. Yet at the same time His most tender and winsome and merciful word for us, the thing we need the most, is precisely His absolute, authoritative "Thou shalt". "Thou shalt" added to love turns love from a feeling based on our shifting moods into a command based on God's rock-solid will. "Thou *shalt* love"—this, as Kierkegaard shows so well in *Works of Love*—is the only thing that redeems love from the fear of failure. For God's will shall never fail, but ours often will.

God shows us these two faces of His love in the opposite way and at the opposite time from the way the devil shows them. *Before* we sin, God shows us the authoritative face, the stern warning away from the incomparable harm that always comes to us and others (for "no man is an island") from sin. If we are sane, if we live in the real world and value things at their true worth, we ought to fear sin more than sickness, suffering, or death itself. At this stage, when we are tempted and contemplating sin, God appears to us as stern and Satan as kind. Satan reminds us then of how forgiving God is, to tempt us to sin and its harms. He tempts us to presumption.

But *after* we sin, Satan tempts us to despair. Then he reminds us of how uncompromising and stern God is and how awful sin is. Satan tells the truth, but never the whole truth. He tells us the truth we will misinterpret. That's how he leads us on.

After we sin, God wants to show us (if we only listen to Him rather than Satan, which is something sin makes much harder to do) the compassionate face of the father of the prodigal son to keep us from despair. Thus we are doubly surprised if we listen to God: first, by how serious sin is when we feel it is not so bad; and, second, by how forgiving God is when we feel only how serious sin is. We should remember these two faces and turn to the one Satan is hiding and God is offering at all times.

The key to discerning God's will is not intellectual but volitional. The heart is the head's educator here. The secret of discernment is *ordo amoris*, "the order of love".

If we do not have this proper order of love, if we upset the hierarchy of things and love some mere thing instead of God as the center of our lives, then this first and fundamental error will generate a second. We will develop an obsession with whatever idol we have put in God's place. No one can treat God as a creature without also treating some creature as God, for we are made with both creature-shaped holes and God-shaped holes in us. We cannot live without filling them. The trouble is, the real God won't fit into the creature-shaped hole, so we have to trim God down to our size. And a creature won't fill up the God-shaped hole, so we have to keep running to more and more creatures to try to plug the gap. It is like trying to fill the Grand Canyon with marbles.

The process of loving creatures as if they were God, trying to fill the God-hole with creature-pegs, always becomes obsessive because we cannot stop and cannot succeed. Obsession always clouds the mind. One bit of beclouding that always happens during this process is that we see God as an outside interferer, someone who is always trying to spoil our fun and smash our toys (our idols). The things that were innocent when subordinated to God become temptations and tugs of war between God and me when I put them in God's place.

But it is hard to discern this when clouded by lust or greed or resentment or envy or sloth or any of the Seven Deadly Sins. We must always hold the line firm on the first battlefield, which is the battlefield of the mind. We must always think of first things first. Then second things will fall into place. We will see the temptation to idolize those second things for what it is: sheer folly. Even if we *succumb* to temptation and sin, let us not *see* it as anything but folly. Let us not rationalize and becloud our own minds to make the guilt go away. Guilt is like pain: a necessary built-in warning device to head us away from the harmful thing that triggers it. Of course, both guilt and pain sensors can become either oversensitive or undersensitive. But they are there for a natural and necessary purpose.

So we must not rationalize. We must reason rightly. We must see things in their proper and real perspective if we are to live well. But the key to this seeing, in turn, is loving things rightly. If we over-love things, we tend to over-value them in our minds in order to rationalize our over-valuing of them in our lives. If we under-love God and people, we tend to undervalue them in our mind to rationalize our undervaluing of them in our lives. If I *love* money more than God, I tend to *think* of money as an absolute need and God as a mere extra. Thus loving and seeing depend on each other. If I do not love properly, this clouds my vision. And if my vision is clouded, I will not love aright.

This sounds complicated, but it is simple when we live it. Say I want to take revenge on someone. God forbids this. Therefore I see God as a bother. But if I first loved God, I would then see that revenge was the bother. When I am in the grip of a lust, God appears as a puritanical interferer. But when I am in the grip of God's love, lust appears as it truly is: a pale perversion of true love and joy.

It starts in the will. If your will is right, if your will is set on "the one thing needful", if your will is determined to obey the first and greatest Commandment, then you will be able to understand, to discern, and to see. Then you will see even the most apparently forbidding and repressive words of God as words of love and liberation, which they really are. You will know that they come from the Father, from the God of love, whom in turn you know because you love Him. If, on the other hand, you do not love Him, then no matter how clever you are, you are bound to misunderstand Him and His commands as threatening to what you love.

The eighteenth-century English writer William Law says in his spiritual classic *Serious Call to the Devout Life*, "If you will examine your heart once honestly and without excuse, you will clearly see that there is one and only one reason why you are not as holy as the early Christians: because you do not wholly want to be." That is another one of those stunningly simple sayings that cuts through the miles of baloney that we manufacture in our mental meat-packing plants. Each of us is, ultimately, just what we want to be. We cannot make our bodies what we want them to be very successfully, and we have only partial power over our thoughts and feelings, but we can make our wills exactly what we want to be in our choice, our intention, our love. We are what we love.

All problems of *discerning* God's will are ultimately problems of *willing* God's will. Once the will, the king of the soul, is subject to the King of kings, then all the king's men in the soul—including the intellect—will follow; and the intellect will discern the will of the King of kings.

I do not mean we must stop thinking or questioning, but that we must use our minds, as everything else, in the service of Christ the King. We must "take every thought captive to obey Christ" (2 Cor 10:5). We moderns have a special block against that, since we worship freedom of thought. But the only way to freedom of thought is to think the truth, for "the truth will make you free" (Jn 8:32). Christ is truth: "I am the way, and the truth, and the life" (Jn 14:6). "So if the Son makes you free, you will be free indeed" (Jn 8:36).

Next to our hearts, our thoughts are the most intimate and important area of our lives and therefore the area we must most invite Him into. For what He enters, is Heaven; where He is not, eventually becomes Hell.

5. Assurance

How can I *know* God loves me? I believe it, or I want to believe it. But how can I know it for sure? How can I get assurance of the most important thing in the world?

The question is an excellent one. It demands something more than the mere mental acceptance of the three-word proposition "God loves me." It demands three greater forms of intimacy or closeness.

First, I want to know that God loves *me*, not just everyone. Me, with all my very specific and very real sins and uglinesses and unlovablenesses. Does God really love me just as I am? Am I really completely forgiven? All my sufferings and failures seem to me to be a just punishment that proves that God does not and should not love me completely because I do not deserve it. I need to know instead that my very sufferings and failures are the caress of His personal, individual love-plan for me, not the inevitable result of His impersonal justice.

Second, *I* need to know that God loves me. I need not just general assurance but individual, personal assurance. "It's in the Bible" or even "Jesus said so" is not enough. Though that makes it *true*, it has to become also *true for me* in the proper sense of that much misused term: I must interiorize this objective truth. I must have what Cardinal John Henry Newman called "real assent", not just "notional assent".

There is a way of knowing that is objective and universal. By this route I can indeed know that God loves me in the same way that you and anyone else can: God said so. There are objective facts. There is data. Christianity is a religion of facts, not just values. It appeals to a public, objective divine revelation, not subjective and private mystical experiences and subtle insights. I can know God loves me by looking at Christ in the Gospels.

But I also need the individual, interior conversion of mind and correction of will and conviction of heart. I need personally to appropriate this objective truth. Christ tells the world who God is; the Holy Spirit tells me. Christ is the public Word of God; the Spirit is the private Word. Christ promises that "he [the Holy Spirit] will take what is mine and declare it to you" (Jn 16:14). Both are necessary. Christ is the Head of the Church. The Spirit is the soul of the Church.

Third, I need to *know* that God loves me. It must be a certainty, not an opinion, a wish, or even a mere belief.

I know that God loves me by faith. Faith is more than opinion and more than belief. It is not even in the same league. It is not even playing the same game. Opinion is the weakest kind of knowledge, knowledge with the least certainty attached to it. But faith, in the Christian sense of accepting God's Word and his promise, is the *most* certain kind of knowledge, for it is guaranteed by the One who can neither deceive nor be deceived.

I need such a guarantee if I am to rest all my eggs in the one strange basket God offers me. For if it is not true, all is lost. If my faith is false, the whole meaning of my life and death is gone. Faith is not an ingredient in my life. It must be the foundation that holds up all the other stories of my life. I need an absolutely sure foundation.

And in the words of the old hymn by Samuel Stone, "The Church's one foundation is Jesus Christ her Lord." He is the proof that God loves me. And His Spirit will give me that absolute certainty personally if I ask Him, just as He did to the disciples, just as Jesus promised He would for all who ask (Lk 11:9–13).

6. Suffering

The most common and apparently the strongest argument against faith in the God of love is suffering. More people have turned sour on God because of that than anything else. If God is love, why do bad things happen to good people?

Once again, Christ is the answer as the love of God made visible. Christ transforms the meaning and value of suffering from something to be feared or at best endured into something redemptive. His suffering changes the meaning of suffering and thus of our suffering, just as His death changes the meaning of death and thus of our death. Our sufferings can become grafted onto His. Paul says so; it is the very sufferings of Christ of which he partakes (Col 1:24).

God's answer to the problem of suffering was to carry it Himself: "Surely he has borne our griefs and carried our sorrows" (Is 53:4). Far from disproving God's love, suffering draws that love down into itself like a magnet on Calvary.

But Calvary's spectacular solution to the strongest of all objections against God's love presupposes that Christ is God, not just another good man defeated at the end. Only if He is God can His sufferings be universally effective for all and for me.

Only if Christ is God and only if my sufferings can be part of His can I embrace them and endure them and even rejoice in them, strange and even scandalous as that may sound to the modern mind. The New Testament and the lives of the saints are chock-full of the joy in suffering. How can this be explained? Only by love. Only love willingly endures suffering. "Better miserable with her than happy without her"—those are the words of love. If my sufferings unite me with Him—the infinitely lovable one, the very source and archetype of all love—if this terrible thing called suffering can thus subserve the most wonderful purpose in the world, our marriage to God—then I can embrace suffering and rejoice in it and triumph in and through it.

My suffering unites me with God partly because it dissolves the glue that bonds me to the one thing that keeps me from God: my own self-will. This is the "I want what I want when I want it" principle that theologians call Original Sin. Suffering conforms me more closely to the likeness of the One who called not His will His own but welcomed every opportunity for saying, "Not my will but thine be done." Saints embrace suffering for one reason only: the love of God.

In a universe ruled by an all-loving and all-powerful God, no suffering should be wasted. The answer to the question "Can it do anyone any good?" has to be Yes. It may do others good rather than myself when I suffer, for we are all one family, one body, and we suffer for each other. But this means it is for me, too, for I am part of this body. What I give, I also receive. If my suffering contributes to the greater health and strength of the body of Christ, then I also *receive* that greater health and strength if I am in that body.

Sufferings do not *automatically* do anyone any good. They must be willed, accepted, believed, offered up, and joined to Christ's. Much suffering can be wasted and is. But *any* suffering *can* do someone good. God would not allow it otherwise.

What, finally, should we do about suffering if we love God and know we are loved by God? What is the practical formula? Simply to use it, as everything can be used, for the end we know is the end of all things: God's love getting its way. Augustine's formula is simple and perfect. Only God is to be loved for His own sake. Everything else is to be loved for God's sake. God is to be loved and things are to be used. God is the final end and things are means. (People are ends, too, because they are not things but images of God. But they are not our final end.)

7. *Love as the Road to Faith*

Faith and love are the two things Christ most frequently calls for in the Gospels. How are they related?

In two ways. The most familiar one is that faith leads to love. Love is the practice of the faith. But the other way is also valid. Love can lead to faith.

I think most converts come to the faith in this second way, through the love of God or of the Church or of saints or of something. Father Zossima, in Dostoyevski's *The Brothers Karamazov*, teaches a "woman of little faith" how she can regain her lost faith through this path. When she was a child she believed unthinkingly. She cannot go back to that. But in her adult life she learned all the alternative plausible explanations of the physical sciences, which seemed to make faith unnecessary and intellectually disreputable. If science can explain everything, is not then faith a mere myth? How can I know that when I come to die instead of meeting God there won't be "just the burdocks on my grave"?

Father Zossima answers, "There is no proving it. But you can be convinced of it." How?

> Through the experience of active love. Strive to love your neighbor actively and indefatigably. Insofar as you advance in love you will grow surer of the reality of God and of the immortality of your soul. If you attain to perfect self-forgetfulness in the love of your neighbor, then you will believe without doubt, and no doubt can possibly enter your soul. This has been tried. This is certain. [3]

Unfortunately, the woman finds it easy to love humanity but hard to love her neighbor, which is the only possible

[3] Fyodor Dostoyevski, *The Brothers Karamazov*, trans. Constance Garnett (New York: Random House, n.d.).

object of the active love, the *agape* that Father Zossima is talking about. For "love in action is a harsh and dreadful thing compared to love in dreams."

The reason why active love of neighbor leads to faith in God and the immortal soul is that our neighbor is the image of God. Love has eyes, and once they are opened we will see our neighbor's soul as a thing that dare not die, a thing that could not die, a thing that could not be replaced, not just in our feelings but in objective reality; that is, in God's consciousness.

For love-consciousness shares in God's consciousness. Love perceives the unique and incalculable value of each of the Father's children. Thus the Father is seen through His children. We see clearly that if there is no God, these souls have no Father, these images no model, these sparks no originating fire, these sunbeams no sun. Thus love perceives both God and immortal souls. If there is no immortality, then the indispensable is dispensed with, the thing infinitely more precious than diamonds—the beloved's soul—is treated like dirty disposable diapers. And if there is no God, then love comes from nowhere and ends nowhere, and so do souls.

The whole argument depends on an insight, an understanding, which you have only when you love. That love must be *agape*. It cannot be the passive love of feelings but the active love of *agape*. It cannot be the "love in dreams" that is like a pillow but the "love in action" that is like God, "a harsh and dreadful thing", but the most wonderful thing there is.

8. *Love of God as the Road to Love of Self*

"God loves you": How revolutionary and how life-changing is that truth applied to the task of coming to love and accept ourselves!

Consider the woman with the alcoholic husband who abuses her physically or mentally and who endures and accepts this situation. Why? Her problem begins where Eve's did: she listens to someone else's voice rather than God's. Her husband tells her by his actions that she is a slave, a thing, a nobody. God tells her she is somebody—somebody precious because she is loved by God. Suppose she starts listening to God instead of to her husband. What will happen? A revolution will happen in her mind and in her life. Whether her marriage will be saved or not depends on her husband as well as on her, for "it takes two to tango." But one, at least, will now be dancing the divine dance and inviting the other to follow. From a zero chance to a 50 percent chance is at least a revolutionary improvement.

If God loves me, I must love myself—not coddle myself but respect myself, not idolize myself but love myself as I love my neighbor. Otherwise, I call God a fool. If God calls me precious and I call myself junk, I am calling God a liar.

"Accept yourself. Love yourself. Respect yourself." This is good advice, properly understood. But why *should* I if I do not feel like it? What is the rock-solid, inescapable objective foundation for my self-love? If it is only my feelings or perceptions, or my psychologist's, then my house of self-esteem is built on sand. When the rains come, it will fall, and great will be the fall of it (Mt 7:26–27). But if it is based on God's Word, which cannot be broken (Jn 10:35), then even when the rains of bad feelings and self-doubt come, my house of self-love stands firm because it is built on the rock of God's Word, not mine. Self-esteem is necessary for all psychological health, and there is no absolutely sure basis for self-esteem other than the assurance of God's love for me.

9. The Recovery of Awe

We said earlier that the disappearance of the experience of awe, worship, wonder, and holy fear was the single most radical psychological loss in modern times. The most blasphemous form of this loss, I think, is the trivialization of the love of God to something like candy, even cotton candy, something *nice*, something *comfortable*.

Thinking of the love of God as something nice is forgetting that the love of God is the love *of God*. The awesomeness of God makes the love of God equally awesome. As Rabbi Abraham Heschel, a great Jewish theologian of the twentieth century, said, "God is not nice. God is not an uncle. God is an earthquake." If you do not like that (one of my students responded to that quotation, "I prefer a God I can handle"; indeed!), then you do not like the love of God, for the love of God is also an earthquake, not an uncle's love, but a Father's.

There is no greater earthquake. It is the "still, small voice" that is greater than the physical earthquake or the fire or the hurricane (1 Kings 19:9–13). This is the earthquake that turned the world upside down (Acts 17:6), turned the sun to darkness and darkness to light on Calvary, ripped the veil of the Holy of Holies in the temple, and shattered the insulation between earth and Heaven. If understanding the significance of that greatest event that ever happened will not restore awe, nothing ever will.

10. God's Love and the Conquest of Sin

We often secretly (or not so secretly) fear that the emphasis on God's love is dangerous because it may make us more lenient toward sin. We think that justice and punishment and wrath must offset and balance love at least a little bit, for otherwise we will sink into an anarchistic orgy.

It is true that we are weak, foolish, and sinful. The "old man" in us is looking for any excuse to sin, even a bad excuse. It is also true that we can and do misuse great and profound truths to our own hurt. So we can also misuse this one. But in my experience it is more usually the other way around: sin comes from *not* realizing God's love. Sin comes from thinking of ourselves only as sinners, while overcoming sin comes from thinking of ourselves as overcomers. We act out our perceived identities.

God's love for us manifests itself supremely on the Cross. How could *that* lead us to take sin lightly?

The more we realize we are loved, the more ashamed we are not to love back. The more we see sin as a violation of love, not just of law, the more powerful a motive we will have to overcome it. For sin is attractive to us (otherwise we would never be attracted to it) and can be cast out only by something more attractive.

Despair of God's love because we are such sinners is further from the truth and a deeper sin than even presumption or pride, says Aquinas, because God is more essentially love and mercy than justice and punishment. Therefore to despair of His love is even worse than presumption against His justice.

The most devastatingly tender poem I have ever read about God's love conquering despair is the metaphysical poet George Herbert's simple little poem "Love".[4] It is a dialogue between Love itself (Christ) and our reluctant, fearful soul:

[4] George Herbert, "Love", in *The Harper Book of Christian Poetry*, ed. Anthony S. Mercatante (New York: Harper and Row, 1972), pp. 134–35.

Love (III)

Love bade me welcome; yet my soul drew back,
Guilty of dust and sin.
But quick-eyed Love, observing me grow slack
From my first entrance in,
Drew nearer to me, sweetly questioning
If I lacked anything.

"A guest," I answered, "worthy to be here."
Love said, "You shall be he."
"I, the unkind, ungrateful? Ah, my dear,
I cannot look on Thee."
Love took my hand, and smiling, did reply,
"Who made the eyes but I?"

"Truth, Lord, but I have marred them: let my shame
Go where it doth deserve."
"And know you not," says Love, "Who bore the blame?"
"My dear, then I will serve."
"You must sit down," says Love, "and taste my meat."
So I did sit and eat.

11. The Secret of Joy

The secret of joy is hidden in the word itself: first J, then O, then Y: Jesus first, Others next, Yourself last.

All who have practiced this have found joy. "This has been tried. This is certain", as Father Zossima said. All who have tried other ways to joy have found something other than deep, lasting joy. With these billions of experiments around, all proving the same conclusion, we must be insane to doubt it.

We *are* insane. That is what sin is. Sanctity is identical with sanity. It means living the truth, living in reality. Sin always substitutes unreality for reality.

Anyone who does not agree with the stated results of the two experiments above has not tried both. All who have tried both God's way to joy and other ways to joy—whether pleasure or power or wealth or fame or whatever—have found the same conclusion, simply because that is what is there. There is only one way to test this bold claim, and we are busy doing just that all the time. At least we are busy testing the second half of the claim, the joylessness of all alternatives.

What if we dared to ... no, the thought is too bold, too terrifying, too radical to think ... what if we actually tried the only other thing we have not tried yet, God's way?

The secret of life is missed not because it is obscure or complex, but because it is embarrassingly clear and simple. We have to be like little children to accept it. A wise man told us that once (Mt 18:3). I wonder whether we really believe it?

12. God's Love, Our Only Anchor

We live in an age of troubled morals everywhere, of infidelities in the board room and the bedroom, of scandals in high places and low places, of greed and corruption in politics and the courts, of revelations of lusts and lies and cheating in the churches. Whom can we trust anymore?

We live in the age of "anything goes", the age of "everyone does it", the Age of Kinsey, the age where half of all marriages end in divorce and three-fourths of those that do not are things of regret. According to an informal Ann Landers poll, 75 percent of the married couples who were *not* divorced would not have married their partner again if they had the choice. That makes seven out of eight marriages failures. In such an age, whom can you trust never to fail you?

Divorce [and remarriage] is a sin not only (1) against God and his law, (2) against your partner, and (3) against the truth (for you solemnly swore fidelity till death) and thus (4) against yourself and your honesty, but (5) most tragically it is a sin against the innocent and vulnerable ones: the children. Rip away all the polite but cruel coverups: the truth is that divorce is always devastating to the kids; and everyone knows it, even those who try to rationalize it. If it is *not* devastating to the kids, that means they are cynical enough to accept it. That is even more devastating.

Divorce is parental infidelity. When you cannot even trust your own mother and father, whom can you trust? "When my father and my mother forsake me, then the Lord will take me up" (Ps 27:10 KJV).

Is that pious rhetoric? No, it is absolutely essential psychological anchoring in a world where there are no other absolutely trustworthy anchors, a world where your own parents or your own spouse may one day let you down. (How do you know they will not? No one who has been betrayed ever expected to be.) In a world of universal moral failure, only God will never fail you. If you do not know that, you will go quietly insane: If God is not absolute love, we are doomed. If Christ on the Cross is not something more than just another good man betrayed, if Christ is not God incarnate, definitively revealing the truth of God's never-give-up, go-all-the-way love—then let's all just quietly pack it up and go home. (But then we have no home.) There are ultimately only two possibilities: (1) God is love, or (2) despair.

10

God's Love in Political Theology: Why God's Love Is neither Right nor Left

What is the worst thing that can happen to the Church? Not torture, murder, threats, persecution, or even the whole world conspiring to exterminate her from the face of the earth. That happened once, and the result was the greatest growth the Church has ever seen. Tertullian's well known saying: "The blood of the martyrs is the seed of the Church" [1] confirms that. Nations where the Church was or is persecuted today—like Russia, China, and Poland—show a far stronger, healthier, and faster-growing Church than do nations where she is established, comfortable, and respected—nations like America, England, and Holland. China welcomed Christian missionaries for fifty years, and there were only two million conversions in those fifty years. The Communists shut the doors and persecuted the Church for twenty years. After those twenty years of persecution there were twenty million Christians in China!

No, the worst thing that can happen to the Church is the thing that is happening now in First World countries, not what is happening in Second World countries (political hardship) or Third World countries (economic hardship). Mother Teresa told an astonished audience at her Harvard

[1] CCC 852, quoting Tertullian, *Apologeticus* 50, 3 (PL 1:603).

commencement address that Americans were wrong to call India a poor country. India is a rich country. *America* is a poor country, she said. It all depends on whether you use a spiritual or a physical thermometer to take a country's temperature.

The worst thing that can happen to the Church is what is happening to the Church now in the West, namely that the Church is deliberately conforming to the world. This is a betrayal of her primary task, which is to conform the world to Christ. The leader has become a follower. The Lion of Judah has become tame. "Follow Me" has turned into "Let us follow the spirit of the age." The imitation of Christ has changed into the imitation of popular culture. Winning the world by converting it has changed to trying to win the world by pandering to it.

Nowhere has this deadly process been more apparent than in the very thought processes and categories that modern Christians use. They are the categories of the world. What categories? The modern world politicizes everything and imposes the political categories of Right and Left on everything. These are the two great convenient fish nets into which all the fish can be classified. They are the two knee-jerk categories that save us from the awful necessity of thinking through issues on their own merit. And the Church is following the tune of this pied piper.

But the love of God cannot follow the piper's tune. Understanding the love of God frees us definitively from the domination of these two secular political categories. Let us see how.

The Right versus the Left

The essential insight of the Right or Conservatism is that of the absoluteness of truth. The conservative mind is clear and hard. "Dogmatic" is the curse word the Left uses to describe it.

The essential insight of the Left or Liberalism is that of the absoluteness of love. If an idea or program seems to be loving, seems to help people, if it is compassionate, then the Left is for it. The curse word the Right uses for this is "bleeding-heart liberalism".

Both positive insights are profoundly right. There are two absolutes because they are the very nature of God. The fault of the conservative is to fail to see that love is also absolute, and the fault of the liberal is to fail to see that truth is also absolute.

The conservative also fails to see that truth without love is not even the absolute truth, and the liberal fails to see that love without truth is not even the absolute love, not true love. Thus each side fails to see not only the other's absolute, but even its own. Conservatives tend to see truth as a hard, impersonal thing, and liberals tend to see love as a soft and subjective thing. Both are wrong. Truth is a person, not a principle (Jn 14:6). And love is as hard and supernatural as God himself. Truth is not cold correctness, and love is not warm wimpiness.

Nearly all thinking about the crucial moral problems of our day is victimized and vitiated by this false opposition. Because love is seen as soft, its defenders teach, "If it feels good, do it." And because truth is seen as hard, its defenders tend to forget love, to demote it from its place of primacy.

The Saints Point the Way to Love and Truth

All the saints escape the categories of Left and Right. They all know a love that is neither soft nor hard, for they all know God. Thus they also know a truth that is not soft and subjective or hard, abstract, impersonal, and doctrinaire. The Truth they know is the same person as the Love they know.

Take Augustine for example. Augustine is probably the most influential saint in history next to Paul. Nearly every person living in the Western world would be a different person if Augustine had never existed or if he had been different. Nearly single-handedly, he forged the fundamental philosophical and theological and political principles of Christendom for the next thousand years, the Christian era.

Augustine is traditionally depicted in statuary as holding two things. In one hand he has an open book; in the other hand he has a burning heart. For no one in history, perhaps, was ever so like Jesus in this respect. He had the combination of a burning, passionate heart of love and a cool, strong, overarchingly wise mind. It was not just the *combination* of these two but the *oneness* of them that was so remarkable. The passion of love shared the light of truth, and the light of truth shared the passion of love in Augustine's words and in Augustine's life. No one can read the *Confessions*, the greatest masterpiece of religious thought and introspection ever written outside the Bible, without recognizing this. (But if you read it, please be especially careful to select a translation that conveys, rather than masks, the passion and poetry. Frank Sheed's is the best. Pine-Coffin's translation deserves its name.)

Knowledge of the truth and love of the good are the two distinctively human activities, the two things animals cannot do. They cannot understand truth or freely choose to love persons. These are the two functions of the human soul that come not from the bodily organism or the environment, both of which we share with animals, but from our personal center, our heart and soul.

These two things are also the two things to which all the saints devote themselves. They will die for the truth, and they will spend themselves totally for love. They are good teachers because they love both the objective truth taught and the subjective person taught. They do not neglect the subject for the student or the student for the subject.

Love and truth are also the two things emphasized by the fifteen million or so Americans who have returned from near death experiences. One thing nearly all these people say is that their values have radically changed. They now see the many things they used to think terribly important as not so important after all, for they do not last beyond death. "You can't take it with you." This applies to everything except these two things: understanding the truth and loving persons. These two last forever. They are the very substance of heavenly life. Therefore, they must be pursued totally and uncompromisingly on earth.

All these people who seem to have shared something of the vision of life-after-death say this in different ways. They do not necessarily become more saintly, more holy people. They do not necessarily practice what they preach (some do, some do not). But they all preach more clearly, and they all preach the same essential sermon. They invariably focus on these two facets of "the one thing needful". The understanding they talk about is always more than factual, informational, and calculating. It is wisdom. And the love they talk about is more than instinctive affection or sexual desire, or even ordinary friendship. It is *agape*, however dimly seen.

This insight into the absoluteness of truth and love and their unity is both a peacemaking insight and a warmaking insight. It is like Jesus, who says on the one hand, "My peace I give to you" (Jn 14:27) and on the other hand, "I have not come to bring peace but a sword" (Mt 10:34). How does this work?

God is love. How can the Prince of Peace bring a sword? Because that is what love does. It is precisely God's love that produces the great divide, the crossroad of history. God's love is not just a comforting, timeless truth. It is an eruption, a volcano, a most uncomfortable deed, a crucifixion.

In this deed is my hope, not in the mere timeless fact that God is love. I am saved not by the beautiful Trinitarian life of God but by the gory death of God. I am saved not by the touching of the three Persons in Heaven but by the touching of this love on the Cross to my life.

The Cross Is the Crux of Everything

This Cross is the crux of everything. It reconciles Heaven and earth, God and man. But it also divides mankind. For it is there at the Cross that we see Love's enemies, Love's crucifiers, as well as Love's friends. At the Cross we see the ultimate warfare. The Cross is God's sword stuck into the earth held by the hilt from Heaven.

It is also Satan's supreme attack and apparent triumph over the God who was foolish enough to step into his trap and into the terrible words, "My God, my God, why hast thou forsaken me?" (Mt 27:46). How Satan must have loved those words! He had apparently succeeded. He had split the eternal Trinity, introduced death into the heart of Life, demonstrated dramatically the folly of love, and even killed God!

But this very event, the deicide, was also the supreme defeat of Satan, the salvation of God's people, and the triumph of love. On the Cross, life triumphed over death through the very event of the apparent triumph of death over life.

Mors et vita duello / Conflixere mirando, "Death and life duel in wonderful conflict", the Catholic Church proclaims in her Easter Sunday Liturgy. Indeed He came to bring a sword and also peace, but peace by means of a sword.

Not a physical sword, of course. He soon stopped that confusion when he commanded General Peter to put up his sword and healed the only casualty of the shortest and most just war in history by restoring Malchus' ear (Jn 18:10–11; Lk 22:51). Christians have been making Peter's mistake ever since, trusting in Caesar and chariots and horses and treaties and nukes and antinukes rather than in the love of God, the love on the Cross. This love is infinitely more powerful than and totally in control of all the forces that crucify it, all the chariots and horsemen, even the horsemen of the apocalypse.

The love of God is so far from being an easy, secure, comfortable, and sleepy love that both the undying ecstasy of Heaven and the undying torments of Hell are made of it. The very same fire that never goes out—by which the saints are blessed and blissed, the fire of God's love—is the fire by which the damned are tortured, for they are its enemies and haters. For no one is this a *comfortable* love.

Lady Julian of Norwich, a remarkable medieval prioress, asked God to show her some of His mysteries, which He did. One of the things He showed her was His wrath. This had been a mystery to her because she knew, both from her faith in Scripture and from her own experience of God touching her soul, that God was pure love. And yet Scripture speaks of the wrath of God, so it must be real. What could it be? She asked God, and instead of explaining it to her, He showed it to her. And she said it was real indeed, but not where she had thought it was supposed to be. It was not in God Himself. She said of the "showing" simply this: "I saw no wrath but on man's part."

The love of God is no projection of anything in us, but the wrath of God is. The wrath of God is real, all right. In fact, it is the very nature of God, the God who is love, but whose love is also absolute truth and justice and righteousness. The wrath of God is the love of God as experienced by someone who does not love Him, does not love truth and justice and righteousness, does not want truth to be truth—someone who will not repent and agree with God, someone who will not admit and stand in the light of God's truth but insists on creating his own truth and his own justice and his own righteousness. To such a one who loves his own darkness rather than God's light, that light is torture. Light (truth) and love are one. Therefore to one who does not love God, God's love is torture. This is hardly a comfortable and easy love!

Living God's Love Is the Answer to Every Problem

All the world's greatest problems can be solved only by sanctity, by our living God's love. The social and political consequences of sanctity are the greatest untapped resource in the world. I do not mean that the saints have some secret political program and should become consultants to governments. Rather, their practice, their lives, their lived understanding of God's love makes other things always fall into place.

But that love, in turn, cannot be taught but only caught. And it cannot be caught backwards, so to speak, from its effects, from those things that it makes fall into place. You cannot get the cause out of the effects, but you get the effects out of the cause. You can get juice out of an orange, but you cannot get an orange out of its juice. You can get new political and social solutions and structures out of sanctity and the saints, but you cannot make saints simply out of structures. First things first.

But then the second things come. Seek first the Kingdom of God and His righteousness, seek first the Kingdom of love and its justice; and then all the other things, all the little pieces of justice, will be added unto you.

What follows are some preliminary sketches, some suggestions about how this divine love that transcends our Right-Left and hard-soft dilemmas might be applied and help to heal some of the most crucial hurts and problems in our world today. These sketches are not meant to be definitive but only suggestive in a few selected trouble spots.

Parenting. No one has a clear, concrete picture of the ideal family any more. The old patterns, the ancestral traditions, the Victorian tintypes, are all dead and buried. Does anyone seriously propose Victorian paternalism today with wife and kiddies meekly and silently sitting at the foot of the omniscient and omnipotent lord of the castle? Yet does anyone seriously propose that in family life "anything goes"? What is the right and natural mean between these extremes? What is a good family? If we do not know, we do not know what is the right foundation of society.

Specifically, should we have more authority or more permissiveness? More discipline, more formality, more law? Or less? Should we be harder or softer?

Perhaps that's the wrong question. Perhaps there is a third way because there is a second dimension. Let us look at the perfect model of love. Jesus is a spiritual parent, the head of the body of Christ, which is like a family. Was Jesus "hard" or "soft"?

Both. But His authority was not force, and His permissive freedom was not indifference. Somehow He transcended the dilemma. God's love has a habit of doing that, transcending human dilemmas.

How? Is there a formula for it? Can someone write a book about how to do it? No. Even good books do not make us good. Good men make good books, good books do not make good men. What does? The love of God. Let the living God into you and He will find a way through the thicket of modern difficulties, like water through sand. The saints find ways. "The times are never so bad but that a good man can live in them", said Thomas More, father and husband and family saint.

How disappointing! You may have thought I was going to give you a formula. The absence of one seems like a cop-out. But it is not; for the answer is not a formula but a person. Parenting is personal. Parenting, like teaching, is largely lovemaking. Lovemaking cannot be formulated like winemaking. But it can be done.

Politics. The same nonformula answer must be given to the question about the relation between Christianity and politics. There is no one political program, no one political regime, even democracy, that necessarily follows from the love of Christ. Each political system has pluses and minuses, attractive and dangerous features. The key to a good society is good people. Good people will make good systems. But good systems will not make good people. Peter Maurin, the thinker behind Dorothy Day's Catholic Worker movement, defined the good society as simply "a society in which it is easy to be good".

To say the system is secondary sounds again like a cop-out. But it is true, for bad people in a society with good structures will make the structures bad or misuse the good ones, while good people in a society with bad structures will make the structures better. It is like putting good people in decaying old buildings. They will improve them. But put bad people in good new buildings and they will destroy them. An ancient Chinese proverb says, "When the wrong man uses the right means, the right means work in the wrong way."

If people were saints, our political problems would be solved. They would not be solved magically, but they would be solved as God would solve them because God *would* solve them. For a saint is simply someone who lets God in. And when God is in, He acts.

Of course, this sounds scandalously simplistic. But it is not meant to substitute for the hard, specific questions, questions about institutions and laws and structures. These are also important. But this is *more* important.

Feminism. Addressing the issue of feminism today is like playing with a hornet's nest. An army of angry, emancipated women who hate the men who have used and abused them can hardly be expected to be balanced, patient, and calm in their judgment. These radical feminists seem bent on destroying two of the most precious things in the world: femininity and masculinity. They will listen neither to sweet reasonableness nor to authority.

But they may listen to love. Bring the love of God to bear on their (and your!) understanding of each sad step of the process by which they turned sour on God's plan for the sexes. Look not just at the effect—the dry, hard, empty sense of anger they feel at the end—look also at the cause, at the lovelessness in men that begat a lovelessness in women. Then you may begin to have a diagnosis for the disease of the war between the sexes. Behind nearly every angry woman you will find a man, a husband or a father, who did not know that the supreme power is *agape*. Not knowing this, the man either pursued power at the expense of love or else pursued another kind of love, a weak love that had little power. Behind every witch lurks a wolf or a wimp. No one who met Jesus ever thought He was either. Again, God's love transcends the dilemma of "hard" and "soft".

Much, much more needs to be said. But this is at least a hopeful beginning.

Christianity and other religions. How is a Christian to view non-Christian religions? The Right says: "We're right, and the laws of logic are valid. Therefore they are wrong." The Left says: "Love demands unity. We must find out how we all really believe the same thing deep down, beneath the logic and the dogma." The Right tends to sacrifice love for truth. The Left tends to sacrifice truth for love.

But when saints rather than theologians dialogue, something else happens. There is neither triumphalism nor negotiation, neither "Here's where you're wrong" nor "Nobody's wrong." Saints do not bend the truth an inch, but they bend themselves out of love.

Eastern and Western religions seem opposed on this all-important issue: is the purpose, point, meaning, and end of religion enlightenment or sanctity? Mysticism or faith? Meditation or prayer? Impersonal transformation of consciousness or personal relationship with God?

According to Christianity, it is the latter. But the love of God and our sanctity cannot flourish amid the noise and egotism and busyness of our Westernized ways. Without the silence and contemplation that the East knows so well, our own ideal of love and sanctity is stunted. The plant of sanctity grows from the soil of silence.

On the other hand, without the Western focus of love, the Eastern focus of mysticism is also weakened. In fact, no one ever sacrificed egotism and grasping and busyness and ordinary consciousness for the wilderness of mystical silence except out of love, out of passionate love. Passionlessness is achieved only by great passion. Without the Western motive, the East's own ideal cannot be attained.

This does not yet solve any of the great philosophical and theological problems: for example, the conflict between the Hindu theology of the immanent impersonal God who is simply The One versus the Christian theology of the transcendent Creator-God who is Person and Three. But it sets up the atmosphere for addressing such problems: one of total respect for both truth and love. Mere respect for truth is not enough, as it is in science, because we are dealing here with God who is Love. Mere respect for persons and love of persons is not enough, as it is in psychiatry, because we are dealing here with God, with objective reality, not just with human feelings.

The love of God and sanctity would transform the great dialogue that began in the twentieth century among the great religions of the world from a dialogue that inevitably falls into the pit of Right versus Left into a dialogue that stands and rises. And as the acclaimed American writer Flannery O'Connor said, "Everything that rises must converge." The only way to true convergence, true unity, is to rise to a dimension higher than the old politicized Left-Right ping-pong game. On the Right there is a pit of hard rock. On the Left there is a pit of soft sand. Above, there is God.

Dialogue out of the love of God is a participation in the dialogue between the persons of the Trinity. In this dialogue love and truth are one and inseparable.

Again, we have not solved or even addressed any specific problems in this field. But we have called attention to a principle that we must know from the beginning if we are to have any hope at all of making real progress in understanding each other and in understanding the truth.

War and capital punishment. The God of love commanded wars and capital punishment in the Old Testament;

therefore, war and capital punishment are not in principle necessarily and eternally opposed to the love of God. Yet Jesus preached and practiced the way of radical nonresistance, the nonviolent turning of the other cheek. He practiced private pacifism. Should the state practice public pacifism either against its own internal enemies and abolish capital punishment or against its external enemies and refuse to fight wars?

I honestly do not know. But I think there must be *some* revolution brought about by Christ in this as in all areas of life. We cannot simply insulate the public and the private sectors from each other and practice heroic private pacifism but wage public wars as usual, as if Christ never came.

Most arguments against capital punishment are sentimental, and most arguments for it are hardheadedly rational and pragmatic. Most arguments for the traditional, reasonable just war theory are also merely rational and pragmatic. God's love is neither sentimental nor pragmatic. It is more than what is humanly reasonable, but not less. What would the experts in this love, the saints, say? What would be Heaven's advice to earth on the topic of violence?

I do not know, but I strongly suspect that we have not said the last word on this matter. Perhaps the Church will speak a new and startling word of love in this time of genocide, terrorism, and organized violence. Perhaps this will be a word that neither the Right nor the Left has yet spoken. In military as well as in economic issues, the Catholic Church seems to be groping or making her way toward such a new third word and path, especially in the social encyclicals of the popes of the last one hundred years.

Abortion. Love of God certainly entails love for all humans, including mothers who choose to abort and including unborn humans. Even if you think a fetus is not a person until he or she develops brain waves, how can you be sure? Would you even *chance* killing Jesus Christ in his little brothers and sisters when you know that: "As you did it to one of the least of these my brethren, you did it to me" (Mt 25:40)?

What will convince mothers not to kill their babies? Probably not law, for at-home abortions will soon become so easy that a law against them would be practically unenforceable. Not argument, not even objective scientific facts, for a mother desperate enough to want to kill her baby is not going to be objective and reasonable. Not intimidation and condemnation, certainly. How about love? How about sanctity? How about Mother Teresa of Calcutta saying this:

> Please don't kill your baby. If you don't want her, give her to me. I will love her and care for her as if she were my own. If we do not have enough food, we will share what we have. If the baby has no arms, we will make her arms, and if we cannot do that, we will be her arms. We will love her. Won't you?

* * *

Throughout this book, and especially throughout this chapter, we have found it necessary to oppose two opposite and equally deadly lies about God and his love. The two lies, like all lies, come ultimately from the same source, the father of lies. They are deadly because they further Satan's strategy to lead souls away from the true God and a little closer to godlessness, lovelessness, and Hell.

It is often said that the devil does not mind religion at all, as long as it is his kind. He specializes in two kinds because errors usually come in pairs. As G. K. Chesterton says, there are opposite angles at which you fall, but only one at which you stand upright.

The Right's picture of God steers close to the edge of the Pharisaical pit and often falls in. In this pit, God is not the just Judge but *just* the Judge.

This picture of God is not the whole truth and therefore even the truth it tells is distorted. God *is* just, and God *does* judge. God *does* punish sin, unless both the Bible and Jesus lie. But the *whole* truth includes God's forgiveness, and the *primary* truth is God's love. Both justice and forgiveness are derivative from His love.

The child or adult who hears our modern Pharisees describe God this way finds it hard to love Him. Prisoners do not love judges, even when they are perfectly just.

If the Right's image of God is "Here come da judge!", the Left's is "I'm O.K., you're O.K." It is true that God is compassionate and forgiving, but the Left often uses this truth as a pretext to ignore or deny the truth that God is just and holy and righteous. Morality is then reduced from a divine demand to a human value system, from "Thou shalt not" to "We find it inappropriate to". The Left often treats *belief* in Hell, sin, and evil with the same attitude as the Right treats Hell, sin, and evil! The Left's one dogma is that there *are* no dogmas, except perhaps that God is nice. And if you are also nice, sincere, and not cruel, that's all God has any right to expect of you.

The God of the Right is always right. He is made in the image of John Wayne or Charlton Heston. The God of the Left is always left. He is made in the image of Alan Alda or Woody Allen. Which is worse? That's like asking whether you prefer porcupines or slugs. It's the kind of question the devil loves to get us to argue about, for a hatred of someone else's mistake is one of the most effective blinders to your own opposite mistake.

The love of God, unlike human love, does not bifurcate into these two categories. It is hard as rock *and* soft as tears, stern *and* gentle, demanding *and* forgiving, not by turns, not by divisions, but wholly and simultaneously. There is simply nothing like it.

The perfect example of God's love transcending our "right" vs. "left" separations is the sacrament of reconciliation ("confession"). When a "conservative" enters that holy place he suddenly becomes a "bleeding heart liberal", for he knows that our only hope is not truth and justice but mercy and compassion. And the "liberal" suddenly *wants* the authority of the Church to be infallible, dogmatic and absolute when the priest pronounces that his sins are forgiven.

CONCLUSION

Augustine tells of a vision of seeing a little boy at a beach scooping up the ocean thimbleful by thimbleful and emptying it out on the sand. Then he sees an angel who tells him that this boy will have emptied out the entire ocean long before Augustine has exhausted what can be said about God.

This book's words about the ocean of God's love have been only a few thimblefuls. No—less. For God's love is literally infinite. It is the shoreless sea we are destined to swim in, surf in, and grow in forever.

The only thing I want to add in this conclusion is the most important thing of all: I want to say, "Please". I want to ask you the individual reader for whom I write (for I do not write for "the public" but for individuals) to please do one thing: the most helpful thing, the most heavenly thing, the most joyful thing you could possibly do. The moment you lay down this book, please love God with your whole heart and keep doing it for the rest of your life. Give your whole self to God and to His images, your brothers and sisters. Risk. Be crazy. Hold nothing back. Don't be reasonable. Don't be an investor. Be a lover.

Tell God right now that this is the one thing you want above all: the gift of loving Him completely. Tell Him you will never let Him go until He blesses you thus. Tell Him that even in eternity you will not let Him go until you are 100 percent love. And then you will never *want* to let Him go.

But at this point you must go to those who see much farther than I because they love far more: Paul and Augustine and Teresa of Avila and Thérèse of Lisieux and John of the Cross and Bernard of Clairvaux and John Paul II and Mother Teresa. They are facets of the diamond of Christ. You understand them by understanding Him, and you understand Him by understanding them. They will send you to Him, and He will send you to them. It is a journey well worth the loving.